Footprints of Black Louisiana

NORMAN R. SMITH

Library of Congress Control Number: 2010917846
ISBN: Hardcover   978-1-4568-2631-4
                 Softcover   978-1-4568-2630-7

This book was printed in the United States of America.

To order additional copies of this book, contact:
Xlibris Corporation
1-888-795-4274
www.Xlibris.com
Orders@Xlibris.com
56390

Footprints of
Black Louisiana

A Respectful Forward For A Friend

I will delight in telling my friends that Norman Smith's book, Footprints of Black Louisiana, is a must read because it certainly is. With the publication of Footprints, I will suggest to them that Norman is offering us a PhD education for the equivalent price of a Poor-Boy Sandwich and a root beer, or a tasty meal at Dooky Chase's restaurant. If you have an appetite (and you should) for large portions of exciting and relevant facts about African American icons (known and less known), places, institutions, and events which are important stitches in the tapestry which makes up the lives, culture, and experiences of blacks in Louisianans since the 19th century, this book will consume you.

Footprints of Black Louisiana is a book rich in details about the history of black Louisiana. Norman Smith has robbed the graves of his subjects and resurrected their importance. He has placed them at the most important intersections and pathways of our consciousness. His mission is to make certain that they will now always be remembered in his melody of black history because he has placed them at our fingertips like piano keys we can play over and over again.

Some of us are blessed to know Norman Smith and his passion for black Louisiana history, his easy smile and humor, his intelligence and knack for getting things done, like the annual black calendars he called, "Etches of Ebony Louisiana". In earlier years he would tell stories about his experiences in Vietnam avoiding booby-trapped body bags, and his recollections of the deadly explosions which would nightly light up the Vietnam sky. Thousands of Asian soldiers would appear from their underground tunnels, only to disappear come dawn. His Vietnamese memories were vivid and traumatic, not to be forgotten. After his experience in Asia, he stayed in the memory business and became a serious student of history, and took on the responsibility to tell us things in historical details of people, places, dates, events, and institutions and organizations we should never forget.

Norman Smith chose to focus on the fertile territory of the state of Louisiana, and dug into the body bags of the Pelican state's neglect of its own African American legacy: the black men and women who struggled valiantly through the home grown war and terror of racial segregation. Norman has made us aware of black people worth remembering and passing on to love ones and future generations.

Blacks know very little about their own history in previous Louisiana centuries, and whites know even less. With the publication of Footprints of Black Louisiana, Norman Smith could become White Louisiana's best friend and help them eradicate their appalling ignorance of their darker brothers.

Louisiana cannot be proud of the fact that racial circumstances made expatriates of and forced out the likes of Louis "Satchmo" Armstrong, Mahalia Jackson, "Jellyroll Morton"(Ferdinand Joseph LeMenthe), Madam C.J. Walker, Huddie Leadbelly (Ledbetter), and Sidney Bechet.

The true gifts we receive from Norman's work are the portraits of other lesser known black men and women such as Lord Beaconsfield Landry, Norbert Rillieux, Oretha Haley, Francis Gaudet, Rev. A.L. Davis, and Dave A. Dennis, and, of course, others.

Indeed, I have my favorites among the men and women mentioned in Footprints of Black Louisiana including the late Dave A. Dennis. Mr. Dennis was the President of Local #1419 of the International Longshoreman Association (ILA) in New Orleans before the advent of the Civil Rights movement of the 60's. Dave A. Dennis was a champion of workers' rights and benefits as the leader of the largest all-black union in America, on the nation's second largest maritime port. His exercise of or threat to use the ILA's strike power as a black union leader in the south was unprecedented. In my tenure as a young longshoreman, I was inspired by his fearlessness and courage. I revered Mr. Dennis the way I would later admire and love Dr. Martin Luther King, Jr. After the passage of all too many years, it has taken the determination and the righteous purpose of Norman Smith to render a measure of justice to the legacy of this otherwise forgotten but great black labor leader.

Finally, I believe it should be said that I consider the publication of Norman Smith's Footprints of Black Louisiana as a crucial contribution to the evisceration of black self-hatred—the most insidious, persistent, an enduring remnant of America's racial slavery. Only a serious appreciation of African and African American history and all that is implied can emancipate blacks from their self-loathing and violence toward each other. To the extent to which white Americans ignores and suppress black history, they will be blinded by their mis-deeds, and continue to drown in an ocean of hypocrisy regarding its credo of freedom, justice, and equality for all.

We should no doubt return again and again to the information in Footprints of Black Louisiana. The black people portrayed in Norman Smith's book are members of our extended, and examples of our best selves. The British historian Trevor Roper once said that Africa had no history worth remembering: Roper was wrong. The proof and the pudding which refutes Roper's hyperbole can be found on the pages of Footprints of Black Louisiana. We are all better off knowing the truth. One cannot overdose on a just and truthful reading of African and African American history, including the black experience in Louisiana. We owe a debt of gratitude to Mr. Norman Smith for his publication of Footprints of Black Louisiana.

Rudy Lombard, Phd

NOT CHARITY, LORD, JUST A CHANCE

Somewhere in the still of a lonely night—
A mother raises her head towards the sky,
and as she kneels down to pray—
She wipes the tears from her eyes.

Lord, I am not crying, because I am a Negro.
I am proud of my heritage from birth;
But as I kneel in despair—this is my prayer
Not Charity, Lord, Just a chance on this earth.

Free to walk among men of all races
With respect and dignity in our daily tasks
Not Charity, Lord, Just a Chance
Is the only prayer that we ask.

Bravely we have marched on foreign soil
To keep America the land of the free.
We have given our all to our country's call
Why has she given so little to me?

With sweat and tears, through the Olympic years
Proudly, we have worn her colors to fame;
Not Charity, Lord, Just a Chance
Is all we ask, in your name.

When the history of the world is rewritten
those who read it will tell at a glance,
that the Negroes' plea always to Thee
Was not Charity, Lord, but Just a Chance.

Wilbert J. Lodrig

JAMES ADDISON HOLTRY
(BUSINESSMAN, CIVIC LEADER, PHILANTHROPIST)

James Addison Holtry was born on July 30, 1893, in New Orleans, Louisiana. He grew up very poor in the New Orleans area. He dropped out of school early and took on a job shining shoes. In 1921, after nearly seventeen years, while shining the shoes of an industrious insurance man, Mr. R. L. Johnson, who recognized that young Holtry possessed excellent salesmanship qualities, Mr. Johnson encouraged Holtry to quit the booth black job and come to work at the Liberty Life Insurance Company of New Orleans as an insurance agent. From this humble beginning, James Holtry made the best of that opportunity to enhance his career. He soon became one of the top debit collectors for the company. In about six months, he was promoted to superintendent and then, shortly, to district manager. His salary was increased, and he was given a commission on all sales.

In the early 1930s, the Great Depression hit this community and the insurance industry hard. Mr. R. L. Johnson and James Holtry decided to risk everything to start their own insurance company. With less than two hundred dollars between them, they formed the Good Citizens Protective Association. Their plan was to provide a burial policy and physician care. They went out and sold policies like never before, and the new company began to grow. By 1936, they had more than $5,000 and was chartered by the state. In July 1947, Mr. Johnson, vice president of the company, died. Holtry became president and general manager of the Good Citizens Insurance Company, Good Citizens Funeral System, Good Citizens Drugs Inc., and the Good Citizens Realty Corporation. The insurance company was the third largest Black insurance company in the state, with assets of more than half a million dollars and eighty-five thousand policyholders. Mr. Holtry was a remarkable businessman with a keen sense of gratitude toward his community.

James A. Holtry left a remarkable legacy in this community. His success was shared through many organizations small and large that worked for human rights and dignity. He gave generously of his time, money, and resources. He served on the executive board of the National Association for the Advancement of Colored People; the Boy Scouts of America, New Orleans District; and the National Negro Business League. He was general chairman of the 1945 war-bond drive that raised one million dollars, and he was honorary chairman of the United Negro College Fund, Dillard University boosters, and Xavier University. His philanthropy was well acknowledged at Xavier University. On November 2, 1949, the university celebrated "Holtry Day at Xavier" on that campus.

In 1950, Mr. Holtry's insurance company sponsored the first televised broadcast of a Negro League Baseball game that was played in New Orleans. He was a devoted supporter of the Young Men's Christian Association and many campaigns in need of a humanitarian like Mr. Holtry. Until his death on July 4, 1958, James A. Holtry was a rare man of courage and devotion to helping his people. His positive attitude about life radiated in his good deeds.

MEDARD HILAIRE NELSON
(EDUCATOR AND CIVIC LEADER)

Medard Hilaire Nelson was born in New Orleans on June 8, 1850. He was educated in the Catholic schools of New Orleans. He was brought up in a family of devout Roman Catholics. Nelson was so impressed with Catholic priests that he wanted to become one also. One of thirteen children, he served as an altar server and became friends with the priests at St. Mary's church in the French Quarter.

Young Medard decided that he wanted to become a priest in the Catholic church. He applied and was admitted into the Society of St. Joseph to study for the priesthood. He attended college in Baltimore before going to Rome for classes. He also attended college in London and while studying for the priesthood. In his studies, he specialized in the following languages: French, German, Italian, Portuguese, Spanish, and English. But as providence would have it, six months before he was to be ordained as a priest, he had to return home to care for his brothers and sisters after lightning struck the family house, killing his parents.

In the early 1870s, Medard H. Nelson opened a private school at his home on Burgundy Street. He taught in French, English, and Spanish in the day and evening, and his students were young and old, rich and poor. During this time, he became a friend to the hierarchy of the Catholic church.

Professor Nelson was a strong advocate of educational and ministerial interests. When the State of Louisiana was threatening to move Southern University out of the city of New Orleans, Professor Nelson got involved. He encouraged the archbishop to invite the Sisters of the Blessed Sacrament to establish a Catholic college for Blacks in this city. He sat on the board of directors to help establish the first Catholic university in the western hemisphere. In September 1915, Xavier University of New Orleans, the first Catholic college for Blacks in the United States, was opened. Professor Medard H. Nelson died on June 9, 1933, at New Orleans. On May 10, 1939, the Orleans Parish School Board renamed the Pailetville school, Medard H. Nelson public school. After fifty years of operation, that school building was closed and a new Menard H. Nelson school was built to replace the old building.

JOHN JOSEPH PLANTEVIGNE
(CATHOLIC PRIEST)

John Joseph Plantevigne was born on October 22, 1871, on a small farm in Point Coupee Parish near the town of Chenel; later it would be renamed New Roads, Louisiana. His mother died while he was still young. He and his brother Albert were raised by his grandmother, who was a devout Roman Catholic. To earn their keep while attending school in Point Coupee Parish, they worked in the fields picking cotton. In 1897, he and his brother moved to New Orleans to attend Straight College, which was operated by the Congregational church.

It was during this period at Straight College that John and his brother Albert both expressed hope in serving God and man as ministers of the gospel. Albert decided to leave the Catholic Church. He joined the Congregational church. In a few years, he became a minister in the Puritan Church in New Orleans. Later, he was assigned to Pointe Coupee Parish to start a new church and school for the Black youngsters of that area. John wanted to change things forever. He wanted to become a Catholic priest. There were no Black Catholic priests in the south. There had only been one Black Louisianian to become a Catholic priest. He was sent to Rome to be trained and then received his vows and was ordained. Once ordained, he was stationed in Africa and never returned to America again.

However, John Plantevigne, while a student at Straight College, applied to the Josephite Seminary in Baltimore, Maryland, to become a priest. He was accepted and on September 14, 1902, he entered Epiphany College in Walbrook, Maryland, for his formal training for the priesthood. He became a standout for his deep religious piety.

After his brother Albert was ordained as a Protestant minister, he returned home. There he began organizing a school for Blacks, but it was met with the resistance from the White racists of that area. On August 28, 1903, three years after he built and operated his school, Albert was shot to death by white racists and his schoolhouse was burned to the ground.

On September 21, 1907, in the St. Joseph Seminary Chapel, Baltimore, Maryland, John Joseph Plantevigne became the ninth Black man to be ordained a priest in the Catholic church in the United States. On the next day, he said his first solo Mass at St. Francis Xavier's Church in Baltimore. Father Plantevigne would be the last Black Louisianian ordained a priest until 1934. Shortly after ordination, he began studying missionary work at the Apostolic Mission House. Fr. Plantevigne wanted to become a traveling preacher of missions and revivals. He wanted to inspire Blacks to grow in their love for Jesus Christ in the Catholic Church. He began his missionary work in 1908 and he brought many converts to the church, but his mission work would be short-lived. He traveled southward giving missions and converting many to Christianity, and he baptized many in the Catholic Church.

In March of 1909, he was assigned to conduct a mission at St. Dominic's Church in New Orleans. It would be his first trip to New Orleans as a Catholic priest and to the city where he decided to join the priesthood. He had great anticipation and high hopes to conduct an extraordinary mission for the Black Catholics of this all-Black parish. But his dream was shattered. The pastor of St. Dominic's Church objected strenuously to Fr. Plantevigne because he was Black and refused to allow him to preach to the all-Black congregation of St. Dominic. Fr. Plantevigne appealed to the archbishop of New Orleans, but his appeal was refused. His superiors then assigned him to Palmetto, Louisiana, but again the archbishop refused to have him.

Fr. Plantevigne became bitter over the racism within the Catholic Church, and he withdrew; he lost his zeal to continue missionary work. He returned to Baltimore where he was assigned to St. Francis Xavier Parish. On January 27, 1913, Fr. John Plantevigne, a broken man with a broken heart, died at age 42. He was buried in the Society of St. Joseph's Cemetery in Baltimore. The congregation of St. Francis Xavier church there put up a bronze plaque in his memory for the great work he did as a missionary for Jesus Christ.

OSCAR JAMES DUNN
(POLITICAL AND CIVIC LEADER)

Oscar James Dunn was born in New Orleans, Louisiana, in 1827. He was the son of a free woman of color, who kept a rooming house for White actors and actresses. He was reared by his mother and a stepfather. Oscar was given his stepfather's last name. As a youngster, he worked with his stepfather, who was a stage carpenter. He learned to play the guitar and the art of public speaking from the actors who lived in his mother's rooming house. The public speaking would become a powerful advantage when he became a political leader. In his teens, Oscar became an apprentice plasterer and a brick mason, and he also operated his own employment service. He was trustworthy and had earned the trust of many in the community.

In 1863, after Reconstruction began, he was sought out to become a member of the Louisiana Republican Party, and he was elected to its central committee. In 1865, he became a part of the Universal Suffrage Association, and he worked to register all eligible Louisiana Blacks to vote and encouraged them to exercise that right. When the Freedmen's Bureau began operation in Louisiana, Dunn was made one of its investigating agents whose job it was to protect the rights of the freedmen. Dunn also became secretary of the advisory committee of the Freedman's Saving and Trust Company of New Orleans. He became a part of several successful business ventures. In 1867, he was one of six Blacks appointed to positions on the city's upper and lower board of aldermen by the Union army general in command of New Orleans.

In January 4, 1868, the State Republican Party met to nominate candidates for the April 1868 statewide elections. Dr. Louis Roudanez, owner of the *New Orleans Tribune,* fought to nominate a Black for governor, and on the first ballot, Francis Dumas (a Black man) received the most votes; however, on the second ballot, Dumas lost by two votes. Oscar J. Dunn accepted the nomination for the office of lieutenant governor when Dumas declined it.

In April, Oscar J. Dunn was elected the first Black lieutenant governor in Louisiana and the United States. Lt. Gov. Dunn was a strong and powerful leader for his people and the state. As president of the Louisiana Senate and the Metropolitan Police Board, Lt. Gov. Dunn commanded much influence in the civic and political community. His political influence grew rapidly as his leadership with the legislature and the state and national Republican Party. When the governor became ill for several months, Lt. Gov. Dunn was called upon to serve as acting governor. During this time, he executed his gubernatorial duties so well that a portion of the Democratic press gave his high praise for a job well done. His honesty and insightful approach to government earned him much praise and respect. This praise and respect also brought him great opposition from the governor and some other members of his party who were jealous of Lt. Gov. Dunn.

It was said that Oscar J. Dunn was also being considered for the office of vice president of the United States. However, before his first term in office expired, Oscar J. Dunn died on November 22, 1871. His sudden death brought strong suspicion that he was poisoned, but it was never proven. The newspaper writers and historians of that era said this of Lt. Gov. Dunn, "His greatest asset was his proverbial honesty." Mr. Dunn was succeeded in office as lieutenant governor by two more Black men during Reconstruction.

MAHALIA JACKSON
(GOSPEL SINGER)

Mahalia Jackson was born on Waters Street in New Orleans, Louisiana, on October 26, 1911. Her mother died while she was young, and she was raised by an aunt. From early on, she was brought up in the Baptist Church singing. At age sixteen, Mahalia went to Chicago to live with a second aunt to pursue a career as a nurse. She joined the choir of the Great Salem B.C. In 1931, she joined the Johnson Gospel Singers. Her voice and singing style made her a standout in the group. She received invitations to sing as a soloist, and her career as a gospel singer was launched. With her earnings as a gospel singer, she became a licensed beautician and opened a beauty shop. In the meantime, the demand for her singing was ever increasing. She began to record her music. It wasn't until she recorded "Movin' on Up" that she gained widespread fame as a gospel singer. That record sold over two million copies, and the demand for her to perform at churches and concerts increased. Mahalia toured the country singing to people of all colors and walks of life.

Mahalia Jackson became one of the most sought-after singers of any type music in the country, for concerts, television, radio, and personal appearances. She caused a widespread acceptance of gospel music. Her powerful voice was heard on radio and television stations all around the world. Mahalia's singing style became a great influence on singers. Musicians, entertainers, and people in public life sought her friendship. She had a very pious and friendly atmosphere about herself.

During the 1950s Mahalia Jackson became a positive force among the politicians of her adapted hometown of Chicago, Illinois, and in Washington, DC. It wasn't until she performed at the National Baptist Convention that she was introduced to Dr. Martin Luther King, Jr. of the Southern Christian Leadership Conference (SCLC). Dr. King asked her to sing at a rally to raise money for the "Montgomery Bus Boycott." Mahalia not only sang at that rally but she became actively involved in the civil rights movement of the 1960s.

Mahalia sang at benefit concerts for the National Association for the Advancement of Colored People (NAACP) and the SCLC throughout the country, including her hometown, New Orleans. As Mahalia traveled around the world, she sang and told of the great expectations of this nonviolent movement. She sang for heads of states, kings and queens. She founded the Mahalia Jackson Foundation to help educate students in gospel music, general education, etc. She was known for her philanthropic deeds.

Mahalia Jackson died in Chicago on January 27, 1972. Her body was brought home to New Orleans. Her body lied in state at the largest hall in town, the Rivergate Convention Center, with an honor guard drawn from the military and local police. She was given the biggest funeral in the history of the city—an appropriate funeral for the "Queen of Gospel Singers."

LOUIS DANIEL ARMSTRONG
(MUSICIAN, COMPOSER, AND ENTERTAINER)

Louis Daniel "Satchmo" Armstrong was born in New Orleans on July 4, 1900. He grew up in the Jane Alley section of New Orleans. He was educated in the public schools of New Orleans. At age thirteen, he was a member of an a cappella singing group. On New Year's Eve, while they were singing and walking on South Rampart Street, he fired his stepfather's gun into the air. He was arrested and placed into the Colored Waif's Home for Boys (now Milne Boy's Home) by the court. Once confined, the music director of the home, Mr. George Davis, challenged him to play a musical instrument. A youthful Louis Armstrong made good of his confinement. He learned to play several musical instruments. The cornet became his instrument of choice. He practiced often, and soon he was playing good enough to the play in the Waif's Home Band. Once released from the home, he worked at odd jobs and played music with some of the other young musicians who were trying to play this new style of music: jazz. For the next seven years or so, Louis played music with some of the great pioneers of New Orleans.

In July 1922, King Oliver, one of his ideals on the trumpet, who was very a skillful and popular musician, asked Louis to play second cornet with his Creole Jazz Band in Chicago, Illinois. Louis then began playing with other bands that were traveling around the country. It was Fletcher Henderson, another great jazz band leader who encouraged Louis to switch from the cornet to the trumpet, an instrument he would play throughout his career.

In the fall of 1927, Louis Armstrong headed his first band. He sang with his band in addition to playing the trumpet. In the spring of 1929, he was featured in a New York variety show that he made his first solo recordings as a singer and trumpeter. They were successful, and he received much recognition for them. In 1932, Louis Armstrong headlined a show at the London Palladium, where he acquired the nickname "Satchmouth," he was called "Satchmo" for short. He had several bands during his career. His bands that recorded and performed the most were the Louis Armstrong's Hot Five and the Louis Armstrong's Hot Seven. They traveled to many foreign countries performing for kings and queens, making numerous appearances in movies and concerts.

As jazz became known as the first American art form to the world, Louis led the nation in the leadership of that music. Soon his recording career accelerated, his recordings sold in the millions of copies, and his personal appearances were in great demand. He had parts in several movies, and he was in demand to play on radio and television programs. He became know as America's Ambassador of Goodwill to the World. Louis Armstrong—instrumentalist on the trumpet—and his singing style have influenced the music industry greatly. This magnificent musician had little fear of death; he often spoke of playing a duet with Gabriel when he reached the Pearly Gates of Heaven. On July 6, 1971, Louis Armstrong died. People throughout the world mourned his death. The city of New Orleans commissioned a bronze statue of him and named a park in his memory. In 1985, in the city of New Orleans, the Louis Armstrong Foundation was founded to preserve his music and that of traditional jazz.

LOUIS CHARLES ROUDANEZ
(PHYSICIAN, NEWSPAPER PUBLISHER, HUMAN RIGHTS ACTIVIST)

Louis Charles Roudanez was born on June 12, 1823, in St. James Parish, Louisiana. His father was a French merchant, and his mother was a free woman of color. His family sent him to New Orleans to attend private schools in New Orleans. Louis also studied in France. He graduated with honors in medicine from the University of Paris, and in 1853, he received a doctorate in medicine. When Dr. Roudanez returned to America, he entered medical school at Dartmouth College where he received a second medical degree in 1857. After graduation from medical school, he returned to New Orleans. He became a successful practicing medical physician. His reputation brought him patients of all races, creeds, and colors. However, Dr. Roudanez was deeply troubled with the racist civil laws and treatment toward Blacks.

Dr. Roudanez became gravely concerned about the quality of life for the Black citizens of the south. As slavery came to an end and Reconstruction began, he became involved in the civic and political affairs of the state. During the 1860s, the voice of Blacks and poor people became the Black press. The first newspaper to champion the cause of the Blacks was *L'Union*. When it was closed in 1864, Dr. Roudanez, his brother, and some of the staff of *L'Union* newspaper established the *Tribune* newspaper.

Dr. Roudanez became the president and principal stockholder of the New Orleans Tribune Corporation. His brother, Jean Baptiste Roudanez, was the publisher of the *Tribune* newspaper. The newspaper was organized for the sole purpose of promoting and encouraging the government to give Blacks and poor people equal rights. The newspaper became a triweekly, and it was published in English and French. It was shut down in April 1871 for lack of financial support.

Dr. Roudanez became active in the movement to improve on the quality of life for the Blacks. He made many personal sacrifices to ease the transformation of slaves into freemen of color. He was one of the founding members of the Citizens Committee of 1892. He fought and provided money to wage legal battles to remove the Jim Crow Laws of Louisiana. This committee tried several times to have the legislature, the Congress, and the courts to declare these laws unconstitutional and render the Black man full citizenship and voting rights.

One of the most widely publicized cases was the *Plessey v. Ferguson* case from which the U.S. Supreme Court rendered its landmark decision embracing the doctrine of "Separate but Equal." Dr. Roudanez and his brother, Jean Baptiste Roudanez, who served as publisher of the *Tribune* newspaper, were influential because their newspaper was an active watch dog of the Jim Crow Laws, and it spoke out against injustices against Black people. The *Tribune* was the first daily paper published by Blacks in America.

Dr. Roudanez was a strong financial supporter of many local schools, including Straight University. He also supported orphans for indigents, the church, the Sisters of the Holy Family and their projects, and several benevolent organizations. Dr. Louis Charles Roudanez died in New Orleans on March 11, 1890.

KNIGHTS OF PETER CLAVER BUILDING
1861-1983

On March 14, 1843, in the city of New Orleans, the French Benevolent and Mutual Aid Society of New Orleans was organized.Among its many purposes was to provide for the good medical health of its members and select members of the community. In 1861, the French Society purchased a plot of land, and on it they built a three-story hospital. It was located on St.Ann Street, bound by North Roman, Orleans, and Derbigny streets.The building was constructed at a cost of $50,000, and it was immediately put into service as a hospital. In 1914, the hospital added on a two-story Italian Renaissance component that faced Orleans Street. During its eighty-eight years of operation, the hospital brought life into the community, and it brought relief to much pain and suffering.The building underwent several additions and renovations during its services as a hospital.At its height of operation, the hospital had sixty-five beds, thirty-five doctors, and more than two dozen resident interns. In October of 1949, the hospital closed its doors, and the building was put up for sale. During the next two years, there would be much interest in the use of the building by several groups in the city.

In March 1951, a new historical legacy began when the Knights of Peter Claver, a Catholic fraternal society, purchased the building for its national headquarters.The Knights of Peter Claver was established in Mobile, Alabama, in 1912. It is the only predominately Black Catholic fraternal organization in the United States.As a service organization, in 1951, it boasted of a membership of more than ten thousand members and a hundred and sixteen councils and courts, nationwide.

In addition to it own use, the Knights of Peter Claver leased office space to many organizations, including the National Association for the Advancement of Colored People (NAACP) and the Urban League of Greater New Orleans. During the 1960s and '70s, several prominent Black attorneys maintained offices in this building, namely, Attorney Alexander Pierre Tureaud, a very prominent Civil Rights attorney; Ernest "Dutch" Morial, the first Black mayor of the city of New Orleans; Paul R. Valteau, Jr., the first Black civil sheriff in the city of New Orleans since Reconstruction; and several other significant attorneys.A most significant distinction about this building was that it was the headquarters for the Civil Rights Movement of the 1950s, '60s, and '70s. It also played host to many important civic and political meetings among the Blacks in the city. It was sometimes used as a reception hall for weddings and small social functions. It was home to several prominent Black businesses including a general construction contractor, newspaper publishing company, a dentist, and many others.

Because of its colorful and prolific background in the area of medicine and Civil Rights, the old Claver Building was designated as historically significant by the Historic District Landmarks Commission.They opposed any demolition of the building because of its historical value.After twenty years or more of service to the Knights of Peter Claver and the community, the building began to deteriorate. In 1976, a new National Headquarters was constructed next door to the historic building. In 1977, the Knights applied for a permit to demolish this grand old building because of its poor and unsafe condition.This request was opposed by many in the community; however, in 1983, the building was demolished.

ST. JOHN BERCHMAN ASYLUM
1876-1975

In 1945, in the city of New Orleans, the Sisters of the Holy Family were organized. They became the first Black order of Catholic nuns organized in the state of Louisiana. Their goals and objectives were to minister to slaves, elderly, homeless, and the ignorant. In May 1876, the director of the Louisiana Asylum for Colored Orphans left the state. The Sisters of the Holy Family were asked to operate that asylum. They accepted this responsibility as a part of their growing ministries.

On August 1, 1881, the congregation purchased the Orleans Ballroom on Orleans Street to house their motherhouse and novitiate and girls school—St. Mary's (the name would be later changed to St. Mary's Academy). They also housed the orphaned girls who were growing and increasing in numbers. By 1889, this orphanage was filled to capacity, and the need for more space was essential.

On March 7, 1889, a fire destroyed the circus tent that occupied the adjoining lot to the sisters' motherhouse, at the corner of Bourbon at Orleans Street. The fire totally destroyed the sisters' chapel with the exception of a picture of St. John Berchman that was hanging on the wall. The sisters had much trouble with the circus and disturbance it created. They wanted the lot to build a new orphanage for the girls. After the fire, they encountered many obstacles in acquiring that property. The sisters began a prayer vigil to St. John Berchman to intercede on their behalf to God for the way to acquire the property and build the orphanage for the girls. Through divine providence, the sisters exchanged some of their properties for that lot of ground, and with the help of Mr. Thomy Lafon, a Black philanthropist, the orphanage was built there.

The new St. John Berchman Asylum served the needs of the orphaned Black girls of the city. Many young ladies got a new start in life because of this asylum, and the work of the sisters. The sisters remained in this building for thirty-four years before the need for space increased. The sisters once again found themselves looking for a larger home to accommodate more orphaned girls. On December 13, 1919, an organization was chartered, called the St. John Berchman's Willing Workers. Their Articles of Incorporation indicate that their purpose was "to solicit and collect a fund for the purpose of buying a site to be donated to the Society of the Holy Family, said site to be used for the erection of a female orphan asylum . . . ."

The Sisters joined with the Willing Workers begging for money. They traveled throughout the country collecting nickels and dimes for their project. They located a piece of property on Gentilly and St. Anthony streets. On January 25, 1925, the corner stone was laid by the archbishop of New Orleans, and the building was completed in January 1926. The new home that was staffed by the sisters brought much joy and happiness to thousands of young girls. In 1967, the St. John Berchman's Girls Asylum was closed. Since that time, the building has been used as a boarding school for the girls of St. Mary's Academy and today it is currently a child development center.

JAMES LEWIS
CIVIC, POLITICAL, AND ADMINISTRATIVE LEADER

James Lewis was born in Wilkerson County, Mississippi, in 1832. As a youth, he worked on a steamboat, and his travels took him to New Orleans where he decided to make it his home. When the Civil War began, he was working aboard a Confederate transport steamer. When he heard of the emancipation of the slaves, he traveled to New Orleans. He and other Blacks petitioned the Union Army to enlist Blacks in the army. They were granted permission, and they enlisted volunteers to form an all-Black infantry unit. He became the commander of a company and was elevated to the rank of captain. Following a short tenure, he became dissatisfied at the manner in which the White officers treated the Black officers and soldiers, and he resigned. Lewis then took on a job as a permit and custom house broker.

In 1872, Governor Warmoth appointed James Lewis as colonel of the Second Regiment of the State Militia. When the Freedmen's Bureau began to work to establish a school for all children, Whites became hostile and opposed taxation for support of education for Blacks. The bureau organized its education department. James Lewis was commissioned to go throughout the state establishing schools for Black children. This proved to be a hazardous task. Once, while he was trying to establish a school in Clinton, Louisiana, he was apprehended by a mob of white racists who were bitterly opposed to educating the Blacks. His life was spared when he gave a Masonic distress sign, and a White mason in the mob appealed for his safety out of the region. His life was threatened many times and the bureau came under much pressure while trying to establish schools for Black children throughout the state.

In 1872, Colonel Lewis was elected to the Republican National Convention. His competence and great administrative capabilities attracted the attention of Democrats and Republicans and elected officials of the city, state, and federal governments. He was elected administrator of police and public improvements of the city of New Orleans. This position was viewed as one of the most important in city government. His outstanding work brought him much praise and recognition for his administrative skills. The governor then appointed Captain Lewis inspector of customs. This was the first time that a Black held that job. In 1877, U.S. President Hayes appointed him naval officer at the port of New Orleans. He held this position for three years. In 1884, the secretary of the U.S. treasury appointed him superintendent of the United States Bonded Warehouse in New Orleans. The last presidential appointment held by this distinguished administrator was that of U.S. surveyor general under President Theodore Roosevelt, 1901-1909. Colonel Lewis died in New Orleans at age of eighty-two.

ELIZABETH BARBARA WILLIAMS
(RELIGIOUS LEADER)

Elizabeth Barbara Williams was born on February 11, 1868, in Baton Rouge, Louisiana. She was the eldest daughter of nine children. She was baptized in the Roman Catholic Church. As a young lady, she was prayerful and outstanding in all virtues. Her strong Christian development led her to seek a life as a religious leader. Ms. Williams entered the Colored Sisters of Saint Francis in Convent, Louisiana. She became known in her community as Sister Seraphim. A few years later, their founder died. Sister Seraphim was placed at the head of her community under the guidance and direction of the Marist Fathers. Their small numbers prompted the archbishop to disband the order.

Elizabeth Barbara Williams (Sister Seraphim) was determined to devote her life to doing the work of God. On March 14, 1914, she entered the Oblate Sisters of Providence as a novice. Sister Mary Theodore, as she became known, stayed in the first order of Black Catholic sisters in the United States for two years.

After leaving the Oblate Sisters, she went to work at Trinity College in Washington, DC. While working there, she learned of a certain priest who was searching for a sister to begin a new congregation of Black sisters to work in Savannah, Georgia. A group named the Sisters of Francis from Ireland was teaching the Black children in the Catholic Church of Savannah. At that time, the State of Georgia was proposing a law that would prevent Whites from teaching Black children. Therefore, this new order of Black nuns would be responsible for teaching Black children in this Catholic community of Savannah, Georgia.

On October 15, 1916, under the direction of Fr. I. Lissner and Ms. Williams, they founded a new order of Black Catholic sisters, namely, the Handmaids of the Most Pure Heart of Mary. Ms. Williams received her habit and was appointed as the mother superior and assumed the name Mother Mary Theodore. They also accepted three postulants into the community at that time. They recruited young women from throughout this country and the West Indies. The sisters took in laundry to generate an income to support their responsibility for teaching at St. Anthony's School. Mother Theodore and her small band of sisters experienced great hardship in Savannah due to extreme poverty and racial hostility.

In 1921, Mother Theodore and her sisters traveled outside Georgia to New Jersey and New York. Their ministry took them in the kitchens and day-care centers. Mother Theodore believed that their community would manage better if their motherhouse was relocated to the north. In 1923, the sisters moved to New York and established St. Benedict the Moor Day Nursery. One year later, the entire community moved to New York to establish headquarters as a Diocesan Congregation of the Archdiocese of New York.

Once in New York, the sisters established a motherhouse and a Novitiate there. At the time of Mother Theodore's death on July 14, 1931, her community had performed many great works for the poor, and they had educated many children to the delight of Mother Theodore. Following her death, the order's numbers increased by fourteen professed sisters and six novices and postulates. Today, their community is still working among the needy.

EDMOND DÉDÉ
(VIOLINIST/COMPOSER)

Edmond Dédé was born in New Orleans, on November 20, 1829. His family migrated from the French West Indies. His father, the director of the militia band in New Orleans, recognized Edmond's special musical ability and sent him to Mexico for further studies in 1848. He studied the cornet and violin, but the love for the violin was greater than any other instrument. He pursued private lessons from the finest masters in New Orleans, such as Constantine Deburque and Ludovico Gabici, the director of the Orchestra at the St. Charles Theatre. After much study, he began to play locally, and he was soon recognized as a master of the violin. His compositions were played by many regional orchestras. Dédé's love for the violin and serious music grew with great delight each time he would compose a tune. However, his progress in the commercial mark in New Orleans as a composer was hindered because of the strong racist climate in the South. With the help of his family and friends, Dédé traveled to France to further study music.

When he arrived in France in 1857, he was given a warm reception by music lovers and native New Orleanians living there. Dédé became popular as a violinist and as a man of fine appearance and disposition. He then entered the Paris Conservatory of Music. He became a student of the most skillful and conscientious teachers available. As a student, he won a number of medals and honors.

About 1860, Dédé moved to Bordeaux, France, and became the conductor of the Orchestra of L'Alcazar. He held this position for twenty-five years. During the 1890s Dédé returned home for many "farewell concerts" that featured many of his local friends of comparable skills to perform in the city he loved so much. After forty years in Europe, he visited New Orleans where he was very well received. Dédé received many honors for his great works. He presented concerts across this country. Edmond Dédé returned to Europe where he died in 1903.

EOLA LYONS BAKER
(NURSE, EDUCATOR, AND COMMUNITY LEADER)
JUNE 6, 1896-MARCH 2, 1971

Eola Lyons was born in Houma, Louisiana, on June 6, 1896. She received her early education in Houma. As a teenager, she moved to New Orleans to attended New Orleans University (now Dillard University).

Ms. Lyons attended nursing school at Sarah Goodridge Nurse Training School, located on the corner of Canal and Robertson streets. Three weeks after graduation, she began working at the newly established Flint Goodridge Hospital. This employment lasted for thirty-eight years. She married and became Mrs. Eola Lyons Baker. Mrs. Baker was promoted to the position of superintendent of nurses, and later the director of nursing of Dillard University. She served for eighteen years as director of the School of Nurse Anesthesia. During her career, she then graduated from Lincoln Hospital Nursing School, Colorado Teacher College, the Mayo Clinic, Johns Hopkins Institute, and several other institutions in the field of nursing and education.

Mrs. Baker was very active in church, civic, educational, and social activities throughout the community. She was a member of Grace United Methodist Church. Her many years of health service to Flint Goodridge Hospital was recognized when the hospital administration named the hospital gift shop in her honor. She was elected president of both the local and National Alumni Association of Dillard University. She was credited with establishing the Alumni Life Membership and the Annual Day of Prayer, which is observed by Dillard alumni throughout the country. In 1954, the university trustees voted her the Distinguished Alumni Award, the highest honor bestowed upon an alumnus.

Mrs. Baker was a charter member of the Dryades Street YMCA; she held membership in the Urban League; the Nation Council of Negro Women; the Women's Auxiliary of Flint Goodridge Hospital; and a member of Zeta Phi Beta sorority.

On March 2, 1971, the nursing profession and the medical community of New Orleans experienced a great loss, Eola Lyons Baker, a pioneer in the nursing profession, died at home in New Orleans.

Morris Francis Xavier Jeff, Sr.
(Pioneering Educator, Civic, and Social Leader)
November 8, 1914-August 29, 1993

Morris Francis Xavier Jeff, Sr., was born on November 8, 1914, in Morgan City, Louisiana. His family moved to New Orleans when he was very young. He was educated in the public schools of New Orleans and Xavier University. His first teaching assignment took him to Lake Charles, Louisiana. After three years, he returned to New Orleans to work with the Works Progress Administration (WPA) in the recreation department.

In 1940, he accepted a position teaching physical education with the Orleans Parish School Board at his old alma mater, McDonogh 35. By 1945, Mr. Jeff earned a masters degree in recreation and physical education. He then began another career while teaching school, working for the city of New Orleans. On January 12, 1947, the director of the recreation department appointed Mr. Jeff as supervisor of the Colored Division of the New Orleans Recreation Department. He became the first and only Black in city government in an administrative position that same year and the school board made him an ambulatory teacher for physical education. In both jobs, he was responsible for developing the recreational and physical education programs, which included organizing sporting games, dancing, first aid, and many other activities. Mr. Jeff gladly accepted the challenge to develop the recreational needs of the Black citizens of New Orleans.

When "separate but equal" among the races was the law of the land, programs for Blacks were under funded. It was at this time that Mr. Jeff developed such programs as the Skate Mobile Derby Day and Teen Camp, Play Day, and Day at the Pool, and excellent sporting and dance programs. These activities brought youngsters from all over the city to participate and have fun. Many of Mr. Jeff's programs are still being used throughout the public school system today.

Morris F. X. Jeff, Sr., was a member of Kappa Alpha Psi fraternity, several social organizations including the Zulu Social Aide and Pleasure Club, United Teachers of New Orleans, and many civic organizations. On August 29, 1993, Morris Francis Xavier Jeff, Sr., died. The city of New Orleans held his funeral service in the city's municipal auditorium. Later, the City Council of New Orleans renamed that building Morris F. X. Jeff, Sr., Municipal Auditorium. The Orleans Parish School Board named a public school the Morris F. X. Jeff, Sr., Elementary School in his honor.

EDWARD H. PHILLIPS
(CIVIC AND RELIGIOUS LEADER)
DECEMBER 26, 1866-APRIL 28, 1949

Edward H. Phillips was born in New Orleans on December 26, 1866. Much of his youth was spent working in the sugar cane fields. Because of this, he had a limited amount of formal education. At an early age in his life, he became involved in the causes of his people. He volunteered for the Spanish-American War of 1898 and rose to the rank of lieutenant in the Ninth U.S. Volunteer Infantry Regiment before being discharged.

After the war, Edward Phillips returned to civilian life in New Orleans. He soon became a leader in his community for civic and social changes. He became a member of the Morris Brown Congregational Church. In 1904, Edward Phillips and his wife, Eliza, joined with Rev. Alfred Lawless, Jr., and a group of faithful Congregationalists to establish a church in a new area. Together, they organized the London Avenue Congregational Sunday School and the London Avenue Preparatory School in a double house located at Miro Street and London Avenue. The congregation later purchased four lots on which they built a new church. They changed the church's name to Beecher Memorial Congregational Church. This growing church congregation extended its edifice and resources to help their community groups and churches, namely, Corpus Christi Catholic Church and Central Congregational Church to get established in their facilities. During this time, the seventh ward area of the city was in its early development and had no electrical services, paved streets, sidewalks, or public schools for children.

Edward Philips and several members of his church organized the Seventh Ward Educational League. They worked and raised money to purchase land for a public school for children living in the area. The school became the first public school in the area for Black children, and they named it Valena C. Jones, in honor of an educator and worker in the church. Mr. Phillips organized the first public playground in the area, and he founded the Beecher Boy's Club from which a scouting group emerged. He devoted much of his time and efforts to young people and to the betterment of his church and community.

Edward Philips devoted much of his life to his church, his community, and especially the children of New Orleans. He also worked extensively with the people of Bayou Teche, Louisiana, where he chopped sugarcane as a boy. He often also pastored a church there for a short time. After his death on April 28, 1949, the Orleans Parish School Board named an elementary school to his honor; and again, in an unprecedented move, they named a second school in his honor, namely, Edward Phillips Junior High School. This was a rare occurrence, but for the dynamic contributions of a devoted civic and religious leader, it was a fitting tribute.

CONSTANT CHARLES DEJOIE, SR.
(NEWSPAPER PIONEER, BUSINESS AND COMMUNITY LEADER)
NOVEMBER 11, 1881-MARCH 23, 1970

Constant Charles Dejoie, Sr., was born in New Orleans, Louisiana, on November 11, 1881. He was the second youngest of seven children. His father, Aristide Dejoie, was a very active civic and business leader during the Reconstruction Era in Louisiana. He was elected an Assessor in Orleans Parish and served on the World Cotton Centennial Exposition Commission, which was held in New Orleans in 1884. Constant Charles was educated in the public schools and graduated from Southern University Normal School in 1898. He and his brothers were very industrious. At an early age, Constant began working at his brother Aristide's drugstore, which was located on Canal Street. In 1902, he accepted a job as a U.S. Railway mail clerk, which he held until 1912. He later entered into the insurance business with a second brother, Dr. Prudhomme Dejoie.

They founded the Unity Industrial Life Insurance Company. In 1921, his brother Prudhomme, who served as president of the company, died. At this time, Constant, who had been working as the general manager of the company, became its president. Under his capable leadership, the insurance company became the largest industrial insurance company in the state. It was so successful that he established the Unity Mutual Insurance Company in Chicago, Illinois. It was very successful, but after a few years he sold it.

In 1925, Mr. Dejoie founded a weekly newspaper. The *New Orleans Herald-Louisiana Weekly* was published and sold for five cents a copy. The people welcomed this addition to the community. They also picked up on its descriptive promotional name, and by popular consent the official name of the newspaper was changed to the *Louisiana Weekly*. For more than sixty-three years, the newspaper has survived and it is still operated today by his family.

Mr. Dejoie was a very active member of the Central Congregation Church. He served on its board of trustees for many years. During the years of his rise to financial prosperity, Mr. Dejoie earned the respect of many citizens of this community. He shared his prosperity and time with the community. His generosity and concerns for civic and social justice were admired throughout the city. Mr. Dejoie was elected president of the Dryades Street Young Men's Christian Association (YMCA), a post he held for more than twenty years. C. C. Dejoie was one of the early supporters of the Urban League of Greater New Orleans. He was also one of the founders of the New Orleans Insurance Executive Committee, the New Orleans Negro Board of Trade, and the National Business League.

The philanthropy of C. C. Dejoie was widespread throughout the New Orleans community. On March 23, 1970, Constant Charles Dejoie died, but the legacy of his dreams and stability lives on.

THEODORE LORENZO MILLER
(PHARMACEUTICAL CHEMIST/BUSINESSMAN)
JUNE 10, 1880-DECEMBER 20, 1961

Theodore Lorenzo Miller was born in New Orleans, Louisiana, on June 10, 1880. He received his early education in the public schools of New Orleans and his college education from Southern University of New Orleans and Flint Medical College where he received a degree in pharmacy. After receiving his pharmacy license, he got a job at Flint Medical College in the pharmacy department. He opened his own drugstore on Washington Avenue at Willow Street and found success as a store owner. However, his desire to fill a void in the face-cream market captured his attention.

Between 1920 and 1922, he used his pharmaceutical background to create face creams and face soaps. He had them patented and packaged for retail on a local basis, and he produced his own label: *Presto*. He then started his company to package, market, and distribute his products. The local response to his products was overwhelmingly positive. His products were sold in Louisiana, Arkansas, Texas, Illinois, and California. He developed his own sales force and became very successful with his products. Each of his products carried his name on all labels "T. L. Miller." It was not widely known that he was a Black man, therefore his products sold on its merits alone. In 1930, the reigning Miss America was quoted as saying that the secret to her beauty was Presto face cream.

Mr. Miller displayed great pride in his community. He was a sponsor of the YMCA Youth Council; the Boy Scouts of America, the New Orleans branch of the NAACP. He was a member of the board of directors of the Lafon Methodist Home, and the Flint Goodridge Hospital of Dillard University. He was a lay leader in the Mt. Zion Methodist Church, and many other civic and community organizations. Mr. Miller died in New Orleans on December 20, 1961.

EULA MAE LEE BROWN
(EDUCATOR AND CIVIC LEADER)
OCTOBER 22, 1909-FEBRUARY 4, 1996

The professional teaching career of Eula Mae Lee began in June of 1929 after graduating from Southern University. After several years of teaching in small school districts, she joined the Jefferson Parish School District. As with all jobs before this one, Black females suffered the most from racial discrimination. After many years of discrimination against the Black teachers of that school district, the Black teachers decided that they must change their working conditions. Most important among the issues confronting them was that of "equalization of teacher salaries."

The Black teachers tried unsuccessfully to press their demands for fair pay to the Jefferson Parish School Board to pay them the same pay as their white colleagues. The Black teachers began searching among their ranks for someone to take the lead for all the Black employees of the school board. Eula Mae Lee stood up and volunteered to initiate a lawsuit against the Jefferson Parish School Board for equalization of salaries for Black teachers and principals to equal that of the white teachers and principals.

When attorney A. P. Tureaud of the National Association for the Advancement of Colored People filed a lawsuit on her behalf against the Jefferson Parish School Board for equal pay for Black teachers, they cautioned Ms. Lee about certain acts against her that would not be nice, and yet she pressed forward. The ugly acts did occur against her, and she was even fired from her job for filing the lawsuit. In 1948, five years after filing the suit, the Louisiana Supreme Court ruled in favor of Ms. Lee and ordered the equalizing of teachers' salaries in Jefferson Parish. Her case became a precedent throughout the state of Louisiana for similar lawsuits.

Though Eula Mae Lee had to leave the South to get a teaching job, she was steadfast in her pursuit of equality and justice for all school teachers and principals to the end. She moved to Washington, DC, and got married when a member of her legal counsel, Thurgood Marshall, informed her of the victory. Eula Mae Lee Brown returned to New Orleans and was reinstated to her teaching position with the Jefferson Parish school system. After several years in the Jefferson Parish system, she resigned to take a teaching position with the Orleans Parish school system. In May 1975, after forty-six years as a classroom teacher, Mrs. Lee Brown retired. On February 4, 1996, she died in New Orleans, Louisiana.

OLIVER BUSH, SR.
(CIVIC/COMMUNITY LEADER)
SEPTEMBER 20, 1910-MARCH 18, 1981

Oliver Bush, Sr., was born on September 20, 1910, in Fazendville, La. He spent his early childhood in Plaquemine parish and was educated there. At an early age, he became concerned about the lack of educational opportunities for Black youngsters. He married and was the father of thirteen children. He realized that the only way to effect change in the many injustices towards Black people was to get involved by changing the laws, and he did. Oliver Bush became an activist in the quest for improvements, in the poor quality of life for the Black people.

He became involved in his community. In 1933, he was employed at the Louisiana Industrial Life Insurance Company. Bush later became branch manager of his office. After retiring from the insurance business, he became the second Black to own and operate a service station in the lower ninth ward of New Orleans.

In 1940, he became an active participant in the community and the civil rights movement. He became president of the McCarty Elementary School PTA and the Lower Ninth Ward Association.

Oliver Bush gave unselfishly of his time, energy, and money to many community projects. In 1951, he filed a lawsuit against the Orleans Parish School Board to allow his son, Earl, to be enrolled into a half-empty all-White school located just across the street from his home. In 1960, the eighty-one-year-old Louisiana law that required separate schools for White and Black children was struck down, and the public schools of New Orleans were integrated. On that first day of school, his daughter was one of three Black girls to integrate the public schools of New Orleans.

Oliver Bush was a businessman and a community leader. He worked tirelessly to develop the successful Lower Ninth Ward Credit Union. He served on the Ninth Ward Neighborhood Council board of directors, the Lower Ninth Ward Voters League, and the NAACP. He was an active advocate of equality and justice for all. He encouraged Blacks to exercise the right to vote, and he worked to help other Blacks to register to vote. Oliver Bush, Sr., died in New Orleans on March 18, 1981.

In 1982, the City of New Orleans paid homage in ceremony to this outstanding civic leader by dedicating a playground in the lower ninth ward of the city: the Oliver Bush, Sr., Playground.

THOMAS REUBEN LEE, JR.
(CIVIC/FRATERNAL LEADER AND ADMINISTRATOR)
MARCH 9, 1918-DECEMBER 6, 1962

Thomas Reuben Lee, Jr., was born in New Orleans, Louisiana, on March 9, 1918. he was educated in the Catholic and public schools of New Orleans. Lee earned a bachelor of arts degree from Xavier University in 1940. After graduating, he began teaching in the Orleans Public school system. During World War II, he worked at the Port of Embarkation. "Tom Lee" as he was affectionately called, was a devout Roman Catholic. As a young man, Tom joined the Knights of Peter Claver, a Catholic fraternal organization. He became a third degree member of Fr. John Dorsey Council # 50, where he served in various offices including grand knight. Tom grew interested in the national affairs of the organization by attending conferences, conventions, and meetings about the organization.

Tom Lee distinguished himself as a Knight of Peter Claver. His devoted work in his council was noted on all levels of the organization. Lee sought and was elected to several local, state, and national offices of the Knights of Peter Claver. Tom Lee rose through the ranks of the state and national board of directors as national secretary. He served his local council as junior knight commander and later as grand knight—the highest office on the local council level. Tom Lee was inducted into the fourth degree division. He also excelled in church and community support and participation, all in the true spirit of Claverism. In the fourth degree division, he served as supreme navigator (from 1950 to 1958).

Sir Knight Tom Lee went to work for the national office in the office of then National Secretary Alexander P. Tureaud as bookkeeper. In 1951, when this growing organization established its national headquarters in New Orleans, Louisiana, the national board of directors appointed Tom Lee its first executive secretary. Under Tom Lee's administration, the national organization grew and expanded its scope of operation and service to its members, the church, and the community. On December 6, 1962, Sir Knight Thomas Reuben Lee died. After his death, the National Conference of the Knights of Peter Claver established an educational scholarship fund in his name. This scholarship has helped many youngsters to continue their education.

ARTHUR PAUL BEDOU
(PHOTOGRAPHER, BUSINESSMAN, AND PHILANTHROPIST)
JULY 2, 1881-JUNE 2, 1966

Arthur Paul Bedou was born in New Orleans, Louisiana, on July 2, 1881. He was born to a large family, which was poor. He received very little formal education, but he was self-educated. At a very early age, he developed an interest in photography. He had great dreams of becoming a photographer, and he worked at perfecting that dream every opportunity he got.

Young Arthur's opportunity came when Booker T. Washington, president of Tuskegee Institute of Tuskegee, Alabama, was visiting New Orleans on a speaking engagement. By chance, he saw some of Bedou's photographs. Immediately, Mr. Washington invited Bedou to travel with him as his official photographer. Also he hired him to be the school's official photographer at Tuskegee Institute. Bedou accepted the invitation, and for several years, Mr. Bedou's hard work and devotion to his profession proved to be successful. His reputation as a perfectionist and an expert became his trademark.

In the 1920s, Mr. Bedou returned to New Orleans and opened his portrait studio. As a photographer, his name became a household word to many Louisianians. He photographed people of all walks of life; he became the official photographer for many Black colleges, universities, and other schools. Most of his subjects recall long waits for a photograph to be then at his photo shoots because he would wait for the ideal time, expression, etc., to make his photographs.

Mr. Bedou prospered as a photographer. He acquired real estate, and he invested in the People's Life Insurance Company. He served as vice president for many years. At his death, on June 2, 1966, Mr. Bedou left a considerable fortune to several educational institutions. His wife initiated a scholarship fund in his name at Xavier University, and since her death, there has been a perpetual scholarship in the name of Arthur and Lillia Bedou.

EDNA M. CORDIER
(EDUCATOR, UNION ORGANIZER, COMMUNITY LEADER)
JANUARY 27, 1897-DECEMBER 20, 1974

Edna M. Cordier was born in New Orleans, Louisiana, on January 27, 1897. She graduated from the Straight Elementary and High School, where she earned a teachers elementary certificate. She later attended Xavier University, where she earned a bachelor of arts and a master's degree in 1941. Ms. Cordier became a classroom teacher for the Orleans Parish School Board, a position that would span forty-seven years before she retired in 1964. She was a dedicated teacher and a strong advocate of equal treatment and fair wages for Black school teachers.

During the Depression of the 1930s, all teachers took massive pay cuts, and the school board promised to restore that pay in 1937. At this time, Black public school teachers with equal or greater qualifications to that of the White teachers earned less money because of their race. In 1937, the school board restored the pay to all White teachers only. Edna Cordier and Veronica B. Hill and some of their fellow teachers decided to demand that the school board live up to its promise that all teachers would be paid, and not just the White teachers. The board's refusal to hear out the Black teachers prompted them to organize the New Orleans League of Classroom Teachers, local #527 of the AFT. Ms. Cordier was elected the president. In 1940, a suit was filed against the school board for equalization of salaries, and in 1944 a court ordered the school board to equalize all salaries. In 1947 she was elected financial secretary of the union, a position she held until she retired in 1964. This organization later merged with the Orleans Educators' Association to form the United Teachers of New Orleans.

Ms. Cordier was active with many community groups, including the Xavier University Alumni Association, the Catholic Commission on Human Rights, NAACP Education Committee, and the Urban League of New Orleans. She was highly respected by her peers. She received many honors and awards for her dedicated service. In 1964, the Orleans Parish School Board honored her for "A Lifetime Devoted to the Children and Future of New Orleans." Edna M. Cordier died on December 20, 1974.

FRANCIS YANCY JOSEPH-GAUDET
(HUMAN RIGHTS ACTIVIST, EDUCATOR, PHILANTHROPIST)
NOVEMBER 25, 1861-DECEMBER 24, 1934

Francis Yancy was born in Holmesville, Mississippi, on November 25, 1861. At the age of eight, she moved to New Orleans along with her mother and grandparents. She attended public school at Straight University. She dropped out of Straight University and became a seamstress. Once, a friend invited her to visit and pray with the inmates at the city jail, and she was appalled by the inhumane and deplorable conditions of the prisoners, both adults and juveniles.

In 1894, she began her crusade to offer spiritual aid and assistance to the imprisoned. She was very concerned for the many Black adults and juveniles who were jailed without benefit of counsel, adequate clothing, or food, and having their spiritual needs met. Her crusade in the jails converted many inmates to Christianity. Mrs. Gaudet became president of the Women's Christian Temperance Union of Louisiana, and superintendent of Prison Missionary Work. She became associated with many prison reform groups, and she traveled throughout the South and Europe ministering to the imprisoned. Mrs. Gaudet married twice and carried the name from her last marriage. She was a moving force in creating a Juvenile Court in New Orleans. While serving as adviser to the courts on standards for jails and prisons, especially for juveniles, the courts allowed her to house some juveniles in her home until they could be properly cared for.

Mrs. Gaudet was an avid reader and advocate of educating youngsters. Her devotion was to saving the homeless Black children and teaching them a skill from which they could earn a living. In 1901, she established Gaudet Boarding School for Boys. It was a correctional and educational school. In 1902, she founded and became the principal of the Colored Industrial and Normal School which was an orphanage and academic institution that was later called Gaudet School. In 1921, Mrs. Gaudet retired and turned the school over to the Episcopal Diocese of New Orleans, and under her leadership, the school became a high school and received the approval of the State Department of Education. By 1951, it was the only Protestant high school in New Orleans. Gaudet school remained opened under the supervision of the Episcopal Dioceses until 1954. Mrs. Francis Yancy Joseph-Gaudet died on December 24, 1934. The Episcopal Dioceses of New Orleans named a community hall in her honor.

WALTER LOUIS COHEN
(POLITICIAN, BUSINESS LEADER, AND COMMUNITY LEADER)
JANUARY 22, 1860-DECEMBER 29, 1930

Walter Louis Cohen was born on January 22, 1860, in New Orleans, Louisiana. He received his early education from the public and Catholic schools of New Orleans. He graduated from Straight College in New Orleans. During the 1870s, he worked as a page in the Louisiana legislature where he gained an appreciation for politics.

Youthful Walter L. Cohen worked as a cigar maker, but he left this to become a customs inspector. Through his affiliation with the local Republican Party, Cohen became one of the most notable characters of the national Republican Party. He was elected chairman of the parish and state central committees. Mr. Cohen was a delegate to every national and state convention from 1892 until his death.

U.S. President William McKinley appointed him customs inspector at the Customs House, New Orleans. President Theodore Roosevelt appointed him registrar of the U.S. Land Office. In 1922, he was appointed the comptroller of customs at New Orleans. This office took in all of the ports of the Gulf of Mexico from Mobile, Alabama, to Nogales, Arizona. His office was only one of seven in the United States which was responsible for overseeing the entire country, supervising seven hundred employees. Mr. Cohen was reappointed to this post by President Calvin Coolidge of the United States; thus, becoming the only Black in the South to have been appointed to a job by four different U.S. presidents. Mr. Cohen was often the target of many ill-fated criminal investigations prompted by disgruntled White Democrats who were jealous of his job and authority.

Walter L. Cohen was the founder of the People's Mutual Life Insurance Company, and in 1922, he organized the People's Industrial Life Insurance Company of New Orleans. He served as the president of the company until his death. The company flourished and prospered under his capable leadership.

He was a Mason, an Odd Fellow, a Knight of Pythians, a member of the San Jacinto Club, and many other civic and community organizations. Among Black citizens of Louisiana, Mr. Cohen was considered a political mentor of the first magnitude. On December 29, 1930, when Walter L. Cohen died, it brought to end an era of Black political influence among Louisianians. In 1931, the Orleans Parish School Board pledged that it would name a monument to the honor of this outstanding leader. On August 12, 1949, the Orleans Parish School Board fulfilled its promise, naming a public high school in honor of this exemplary citizen of New Orleans.

FLORENCE EVELYN JOHNSON CHESTER
(EDUCATOR AND COMMUNITY LEADER)
OCTOBER 4, 1857-JUNE 15, 1944

Florence Evelyn Johnson was born on October 4, 1857, in Natchez, Mississippi. She received her early education in Natchez. She moved to New Orleans, Louisiana, in 1870 to attend Straight Normal School and Peabody Normal School. In 1875, she was a member of the first graduating class of Straight College. Her professional training continued throughout her teaching career by completing courses at such institutions as Cheyney State Teacher's College, Tuskegee Institute in Alabama, and several other schools. The majority of her training was in the field of education and school administration.

In 1884, Ms. Johnson returned to New Orleans. She married Mr. T. Morris Chester, a civic and political leader. Mrs. Chester began working in the public school system as a classroom teacher. In 1915, after teaching assignments in several public schools of New Orleans, she was elected principal of Peter S. Lawton School. Her hard work and training in the classroom prepared her for the duties of principalship, but her dedication and commitment to helping the less fortunate was the major influence in her life and that of her husband's.

Mrs. Chester's dedication to educating the children of this community was not confined to general education only but also to religious training as well. Her workplace did not begin and end in the classroom; she went out into the community to teach the word of God. She taught Sunday school to the children confined to Milne Boys Home, to inmates confined to the Parish Prison and to shut-ins. She always had time to talk with young girls about the virtues of becoming a lady and a mother.

Mrs. Chester was an enthusiastic member of the Central Congregational Church. She served in nearly every position in the church that a woman was allowed. She was a founder and the first president of the board of directors of the first day-care center for Blacks in New Orleans, named the Hume Child Development Service.

After fifty years of service, Mrs. Chester retired from the Orleans Parish school system. She died on June 15, 1944. Her death was a great loss to the community. Her good deeds and service to her community will always be remembered for years to come. On December 18, 1959, the Orleans Parish School Board dedicated a new public school and named it "Florence J. Chester" in her honor for her unselfish devotion, nurturing, and caring for all who were in need.

DANIEL ELLIS BYRD
(CIVIC AND COMMUNITY LEADER)
JANUARY 3, 1910-MARCH 18, 1984

Daniel Ellis Byrd was born in Phillips County, Arkansas, on January 3, 1910. When he was ten years old, his parents moved to Gary, Indiana, where he received his early education. In 1935, Byrd earned a bachelor of arts degree from Northwestern University. In 1936, he played professional basketball with the Harlem Globetrotters Basketball Team. In 1937, he moved to New Orleans, Louisiana, and began working as an insurance agent. He became a member of the New Orleans branch of the National Association for the Advancement of Colored People (NAACP) and became involved in the struggle for social justice in the New Orleans community.

After much hard work and dedication to the cause of justice, his efforts were recognized by the membership of the local branch. He was later appointed executive secretary of the New Orleans branch. He became the first president of the Louisiana State Conference of NAACP branches. During his administration, the number of branches in the conference increased in units from three to forty-five. Later he became coordinator of NAACP branches in the southern region. He was one of the founders of the New Orleans *Sentinel* newspaper which was published from 1940 to 1942.

Mr. Byrd worked closely with Attorney A. P. Tureaud on many cases for the NAACP. He aided in the lawsuit of *Joseph McKelpin v. Orleans Parish School Board*, for equalization of Orleans public school teachers' salaries and on many other cases throughout the South for much of the same cause. In later years, they also successfully sued for equal accommodation of public facilities for Blacks. As a result of his dedication to the causes, he was appointed a special consultant to the Louisiana Educators Association (LEA) and the National Council of Officers of State Teachers Association.

In 1946, he served on a team with Attorney Alexander P. Tureaud and John E. Rousseau, which investigated the "blow torch" lynching in Minden, Louisiana. They worked on the landmark voter registration case of *Hall v. Nagel* of St. John Parish. In 1947, he was appointed to the professional staff of the NAACP as a regional coordinator. In 1950 now Supreme Court Justice Thurgood Marshall appointed Byrd Field secretary of the NAACP Legal Defense and Educational Fund, Inc. Mr. Byrd's new responsibilities took him to many cities around the country. Often his life was threatened and at great risk, but he performed his job and served his people well.

Dan Byrd and his wife, Mildred Cage Byrd, were both very active members of the NAACP. She was the organizer of the Louisiana NAACP Youth Council, and together, they devoted their efforts to the cause of freedom. When Daniel Ellis Byrd died on March 18, 1984, the NAACP lost a great champion of justice.

ROBERT ELIZA JONES
(RELIGIOUS, COMMUNITY LEADER, AND PHILANTHROPIST)
FEBRUARY 19, 1872-MAY 18, 1960

Robert Eliza Jones was born on February 19, 1872, in Greensboro, North Carolina, where he received his early education. He then began to study for the ministry in the Methodist Church. In 1891, he became a licensed preacher in Leaksville, North Carolina. During the next five years, he underwent extensive training on the university level, earning several degrees. Continuing his training in the Methodist Episcopal Church, he received a doctor of divinity degree from New Orleans University in 1901.

In 1901, he married Valena C. McArthur of Bay St. Louis, Mississippi, who was an educator in the local schools. In 1904, they moved to New Orleans where she worked in the public-school system and Rev. Jones assumed ministerial duties. Their union produced three children. They worked together on many community endeavors to enhance the Black people of the community. As the editor of the *Southwest Christian Advocate*, Rev. Jones and his wife also worked together to produce this publication until her death in 1917.

In 1920, Rev. Jones was elected bishop of the Methodist Episcopal Church, thus becoming its first Black bishop. He was then assigned to the New Orleans area. In 1921, he married for a second time and raised another family.

Bishop Jones became the first Black elevated to the position of general superintendent of the Methodist Episcopal Church in Louisiana in 1923. As general superintendent, Bishop Jones organized "Penny Clubs" to generate the funds to build Gulfside Methodist Assembly Center on seven hundred thirty-eight acres of land in Waveland, Mississippi. He envisioned Gulfside as a religious resort for Black people. This facility, consisting of several buildings, was used to train men in the doctrines of the church. The facility was also used as an educational, recreational, and cultural center for the entire community. This serene and peaceful resort became the pride of the Black community in the south. The administration building on the campus is named in his honor.

Bishop Jones was very active in local and regional affairs. He was elected the first president of the Negro Business League in Louisiana. He participated in the negotiations to merge New Orleans University and Straight University into the newly formed Dillard University. He was elected treasurer of the founding board of directors of Dillard University, in New Orleans. Bishop Jones served as chairman of the Dryades Street YMCA for more than twenty years. He donated money to many of the projects of the YMCA and to many other worthy causes.

Bishop Jones was given awards, honors, and recognition for his work in organizing and furthering the educational, social, and religious life of the people of his community. On May 18, 1960, Bishop Robert E. Jones died at Flint Goodridge Hospital of New Orleans. He was buried on the grounds at Gulfside Assembly, Waveland, Mississippi.

ELIZABETH MARY "LIZZIE MILES" LANDREAUX PAJAUDE
(BLUES AND JAZZ SINGER)
MARCH 31, 1895-MARCH 17, 1963

Elizabeth Mary Landreaux was born in the French Quarter of New Orleans, Louisiana, on March 31, 1895. She was educated in the public schools of New Orleans. While attending catechism classes, Elizabeth began singing hymns. She was particularly influenced by her mother, who was also a singer, but her greatest influence came from her catechism teacher. She began singing in the church choir at an early age, and she loved to sing and dance at house parties.

At age fifteen, Lizzie, as she was affectionately called, left home to go on the road to sing. She spoke fluent Creole-French, which was an asset when she traveled to France to sing. During the 1920s, she became an international sensation in France. It is believed that she was the first Black woman from the United States to be recognized as a jazz-and-blues singer. Her audience called her "La Rose Noire de Paris" (the Black Rose of Paris) and some called her "the Creole Songbird." When she returned to the United States, she sang in many of the northern cities with many of the great jazz musicians of that time, including Jelly Roll Morton, Bunk Johnson, King Oliver, Fats Waller, and Armand J. Piron.

In 1923, she was the first Black singer to make a record in France. That recording, "You're Always Messing Around with My Man," became a jazz classic. She made several recordings with many of the bands that she worked with. Lizzie's stature was large, and her voice was described as one of the most powerful of all of her contemporary blues singers. She became a landmark at home in many of the dance halls, jazz clubs, and wherever music was the major attraction in New Orleans. She also worked for a short time as a feature singer in a circus.

In 1957, she appeared on a nationally televised program with Louis Armstrong and several other top entertainers. She married twice but had no children. In 1959, she retired from her career as an entertainer. Lizzie chose to live a lifestyle that brought her closer to the Catholic Church. She said that she wanted to devote her final years to "pray for these troubled times." On Sunday, March 17, 1963, shortly after attending Mass, Lizzie Miles died at the Thomy Lafon Nursing Home, where she was praying for peace.

LORD BEACONSFIELD LANDRY
(PHYSICIAN, CIVIC LEADER, AND SOLOIST)
MARCH 11, 1878-JANUARY 21, 1934

Lord Beaconsfield Landry was born in Donaldsonville, Louisiana. His father, Pierre Landry, was a minister, an educator, and the first Black mayor of Donaldsonville, Louisiana. He received his early education in Donaldsonville and, afterwards, was sent to Gilbert Academy in Baldwin, Louisiana. While a student, the president of the academy became interested in young Landry's singing voice. Upon graduation, he encouraged Lord Beaconsfield to attend Fisk University at Nashville, Tennessee, to earn a degree in music. While in attendance, he became a member of the world famous Fisk Jubilee Singers which traveled throughout the world to sing and raise funds to operate Fisk University. Later, he entered Meharry Medical College, where he received his M.D. in 1908.

After graduating from Meharry Medical College, Dr. Landry settled in Algiers, Louisiana and began practicing medicine. Dr. Landry was interested in helping the less fortunate to learn more about taking better care of their healthful needs. In the May 8, 1926, edition of the *Louisiana Weekly*, the first of many articles appeared in his column "How to Keep Well." He wrote for the weekly until his death. Dr. Landry's articles touched on nearly every subject one should be knowledgeable about to maintain a healthy body and a good attitude about one's body.

Dr. Landry devoted much of his service and time to the needy and the poor who benefited from his professional services. He operated a free clinic for some time for the poor people of Algiers, Louisiana.

Singing was the avocation of Dr. Landry. He was a founding member and director of the Osceola Five—an all-male group. This vocal group specialized in educational, religious, and Black cultural songs.

On January 21, 1934, Dr. Lord Beaconsfield Landry died. On May 18, 1938, the Orleans Parish School Board named a new high school in Algiers in his honor for the services rendered to that community.

Archibal Ebenezer Perkins
(Educator, Author, and Civic Leader)
June 21, 1879-April 19, 1946

Archibal Ebenezer Perkins was born on June 21, 1879, on a farm in Amite County, Mississippi. He attended the rural schools of that area. In 1906, he earned a degree from Alcorn A & M College. From 1906 to 1911 he was the principal of the Biloxi public school in Biloxi, Mississippi. In 1911, he returned to Alcorn A & M College to serve as the chairman of the biology department. In 1923, he moved to New Orleans and was elected a supervising principal in the public-school system. He later served for twenty years as principal of R.T. Danneel School.

In addition to his career as an educator, Mr. Perkins was an active civic leader, an author, and a devout member of the African Methodist Episcopal Church. He authored several books ranging from church spirituals to biographical studies. He contributed several articles to the *Journal of Negro History*. Mr. Perkins was quoted several times in W. E. B. DuBois' *Black Reconstruction in America 1860-1880*. He wrote *A Brief History of the Negro in Louisiana*, *Negro Spirituals from the Far South*, and edited *Who's Who in Colored Louisiana*. Several other national magazines published his articles, which earned him the respect of his colleagues who addressed him as Professor Perkins.

In 1934, he was invited to the White House by President F. D. Roosevelt to deliver a scroll containing signatures from the Black citizens of New Orleans, demanding that the Federal Government provide fair and equal accommodations for Blacks. He served as the president of the Young Men's Christian Association (YMCA) of New Orleans.

In 1942, Wilberforce University in Xania, Ohio, recognized his contributions to education and his community and awarded Professor Perkins an Honorary Doctor of Laws. In 1946, Dr. Perkins retired from the Orleans Parish school system, and shortly after his retirement, Archibal Ebenezer Perkins passed away on April 19, 1946.

GERTRUDE POCTE GEDDES WILLIS
(FUNERAL DIRECTOR, INSURANCE PIONEER, AND CIVIC LEADER)
MARCH 9, 1878-FEBRUARY 20, 1970

Gertrude Pocte was born in New Orleans, Louisiana, on March 9, 1878. She was educated in the public schools of New Orleans. She married Clem J. Geddes, a mortician who was cofounder of the Geddes & Moss Undertaking Parlor in New Orleans. After his death in 1913, she continued to work in the business with her partner, Arnold L. Moss. Together they established their own Industrial Insurance Company, which grew and became very successful.

She began a pioneering journey among the women of her community. She enhanced the funeral home's relationship with the community by getting involved with many causes and performing worthy deeds.

In 1919, she married Dr. William A. Willis, a dentist and businessman, and again, her business underwent a reorganization as her husband became a part of the business. After the death of her partner, Arnold L. Moss, she renamed the funeral home, "Gertrude Geddes Willis Funeral Home." A burial insurance company was added, which provided dignified funeral services and burials at an affordable rate through her own burial insurance plan. She increased services and provided more jobs for people in the funeral home and the insurance business.

Gertrude Geddes Willis became a true pioneer and role model among businesswomen in Louisiana. Her businesses were successful, and they grew to great proportions. As president of the board of directors of both businesses, she earned the respect of her peers. Their insurance company became one of the largest companies of its kind in the country.

Once each year, the entire firm would attend a church service together and give thanks for the success of the business. The success of the business was shared with the community through her involvement and participation in various civic and community organizations. Geddes and Moss Funeral Home played an important part in the early development of the Zulu Social Aid & Pleasure Club's annual parade. The Zulu's annual Mardi Gras Day parade pauses at the funeral home to toast its queen with champagne. This tradition has existed for more than sixty years.

As an innovative businesswoman, Gertrude Geddes Willis was very active in many business-related regional, fraternal, and cultural organizations—to those she made many contributions. Gertrude Pocte Geddes Willis, a pioneer of the funeral and insurance industry, died in New Orleans on February 20, 1970.

GEORGE W. LUCAS
(PHYSICIAN/CIVIC LEADER)

George W. Lucas was born in Lee County, Texas. After finishing Paul Quinn College in Waco, Texas, he moved to New Orleans to attend Flint Medical College, where he received a degree in medicine. After receiving his medical degree, he decided to practice medicine in New Orleans. Dr. Lucas stayed there throughout his career. He became involved in the plight of the Black people of the city and immediately joined several of the local organizations which were fighting for human rights. Among the organizations which he joined was the New Orleans branch of the National Association for the Advancement of Colored People (NAACP).

Dr. Lucas was devoted to the cause of his people, and the members of the branch recognized his abilities and commitment to human rights by electing him president of the New Orleans branch of the NAACP. In 1926, Dr. Lucas brought the New Orleans branch of the NAACP to the nation's attention when he led the fight in a court case called the *New Orleans Segregation Case.* The NAACP challenged a code which was passed by the Louisiana legislature and the city of New Orleans called the Residential Segregation Law. The law restricted Blacks from living in White residential neighborhoods unless the Whites had given permission in writing.

In Dr. Lucas's judgment, that law discriminated against Blacks and was therefore unconstitutional. In preparation for this very controversial and highly publicized court challenge, Dr. Lucas raised $10,000, which was needed for the legal fees. The NAACP lost its case in the state courts. They appealed to the United States Supreme Court, which ruled in their favor and declared the law unconstitutional.

The national office was pleased with Dr. Lucas, and they elected him to their national board of directors. He also served as vice president of the Dryades Street YMCA; he was medical director and a member of the People's Life Insurance Company; he was deputy grand master of the St. John Grand Lodge and a member of the Elks, Knights of Pythias, and the Odd Fellows. Dr. Lucas died on January 11, 1931, at his home in New Orleans.

JAMES EDWARD GAYLE
(BUSINESSMAN/CHURCH AND CIVIC LEADER)
NOVEMBER 25, 1892-MARCH 26, 1963

James Edward Gayle was born in Natchez, Mississippi. When he was just an infant, his parents moved to New Orleans. He was educated in the public schools and graduated from Straight College in New Orleans. His participation in the community included an active involvement in the Baptist Church and its organizations, human rights, music, politics, and a successful business.

Mr. Gayle became a member of St. Mark's Fourth Baptist Church. He served as chairman of the trustees board and minister of music. He worked faithfully in the church and was elected president of the First Baptist Laymen Movement, the BYPU, and several other church-related organizations. His works as a Baptist layman gained him recognition nationwide, and he was frequently called on to serve on national boards and committees with leaders of the Baptist Church. In 1939, Mr. Gayle was invited to deliver a speech on a national radio hookup. He spoke on his favorite subject: the potential manpower of the Negro church. He often spoke on radio and to church audiences on the subject of the Black male and the church.

James E. Gayle was known throughout the New Orleans community for his active work for social and civic equality, in addition to the church. He was a founder and director of the Louisiana Weekly Educational Fund, Inc.

Mr. Gayle was a strong community leader who led with hard work and was dedicated to making his community a better place to live. His service to his community included serving as president of the board of directors of the Dryades Street YMCA, a board member of the New Orleans branch of NAACP; the Urban League of Greater New Orleans; the Times Picayune Doll and Toy Fund; and many other organizations. One of Mr. Gayle's favorite hobbies was singing spirituals. He was part of a singing quartet, and also organized his own singing group known as the Gayle Singers. He was a founding member of the B-Sharp Music Club. For many years he produced an annual citywide gospel concert. One year, he conducted the five hundred member choir as they sang his rendition of the Broadway musical *Cabin in the Sky*.

For many years, he operated his own business, James E. Gayle & Sons Music Publishers and Book Distributors. For twenty years, he was the manager of the Prythian Temple Building on Saratoga and Gravier streets. Mr. Gayle was recognized and honored by many citizens and organizations for his contributions. On March 26, 1963, the New Orleans community mourned the death of James Edward Gayle, a great and courageous leader.

ALICE NELSON-DUNBAR
(POET, JOURNALIST, ACTIVIST)
JULY 19, 1875-SEPTEMBER 18, 1935

Alice Ruth (Moore) Dunbar-Nelson was born in New Orleans on July 19, 1875. She has been called a complete writer, poet, critic, dramatist, editor, essayist, journalist, lyricist, novelist, short story writer, and an educator. Her writings and speeches covered a broad array of topics. Many were on the history of New Orleans and the South. Most of her essays dealt with people of color in Louisiana and the Black man's struggle for survival. She was also a committed suffragist and anti-lynching crusader.

She married Paul Laurence Dunbar, the famous writer, and this union lasted eight years. She retained his name, Dunbar, after they were separated. She later married Robert Nelson. At one time, they owned the Douglass Publishing Co. of Pennsylvania.

In addition to her literary activities, Dunbar-Nelson was a school teacher, social worker, parole officer, platform lecturer, and a licensed evangelist. From the late 1890s to the 1920s her literary works were published in many newspapers and magazines across the country. In 1928, she became executive secretary of the Interracial Peace Committee.

Her works include a volume of short stories such as, "Violets," "Goodness of St. Rocque," and a host of essays including "Negro Literature for Negro Pupils, People of Color in Louisiana, Part I & II." Her love for her people and peace in this world can be found in all of her works, words, and actions.

NORBERT RILLIEUX
(SCIENTIST, ENGINEER, AND INVENTOR)
MARCH 17, 1806-OCTOBER 8, 1894

Norbert Rillieux was born in New Orleans on March 17, 1806. His father, Vincent Rillieux, was an engineer and inventor who recognized Norbert's exceptional ability and sent him to Paris for formal training in engineering. He showed rare aptitude for engineering, and by 1830, he was an instructor in applied mechanics and had published several papers on "steam-engine work and steam economy." In 1834, he produced his first practical evaporator system, as it was called; it was designed to crystallize sugar liquors. Following this venture, he speculated in land and earned a fortune, which he invested in his projects. His reputation reached home, and an owner of a new sugar refinery in New Orleans sent for him to supervise production.

In 1845, after much rejection because of his race, his first successful factory-scale pan evaporation apparatus was installed and recognized as revolutionizing the manufacture of sugar. In a few years, his inventions were used around the world.

He developed a drainage plan for the city of New Orleans, but the legislature refused his plan because of his race. Disheartened, he returned to Paris where he became head of the engineering school he attended as a boy. In later years, he traveled to Egypt to pursue the study of Egyptology, which deals with the culture and artifacts of the ancient Egyptian civilization.

Norbert Rillieux died in Paris on October 8, 1894. After his death, there was little mentioned of him in the major reference sources in the libraries and periodicals, and it is believed that he was omitted because he was a Negro. In 1934, a group of worldwide sugar engineers commissioned a bronze plaque to pay homage to this great inventor and donated it to the Louisiana State Museum, New Orleans. The Jefferson Parish school system named a school in his honor.

JOSEPH SAMUEL CLARK
(EDUCATOR/UNIVERSITY PRESIDENT)
JUNE 7, 1871-OCTOBER 27, 1944

Joseph Samuel Clark was born in Bienville Parish, near Sparta, Louisiana, on June 7, 1871. His name at birth was Josiah, but he later renamed himself Joseph Samuel. He was reared by deeply religious grandparents. Enterprising and strong willed, he worked at odd jobs and attended school. He earned a normal school diploma while at Coleman College, Gibsland, Louisiana, and later served on its board of directors. He began his teaching career along with odd jobs to sustain himself and his sister. He later attended several colleges and universities throughout the U.S.

In July 1913, having served the previous twelve years as president of Baton Rouge College and six years as president of the Louisiana State Colored Teachers Association, Clark became the sixth president of Louisiana's Southern University and Agricultural and Mechanical College, a Black land-grant institution. Under Clark's leadership, the school relocated from New Orleans to Scotlandville. The next twenty-five years would see progress and growth at Southern University that would make it the largest predominantly Black university in the U.S. After his death in 1944, he was succeeded as president by his son, Felton G. Clark.

CHARLES EDMUND NASH
CONGRESSMAN
MAY 23, 1844-JUNE 21, 1913

Charles Edmund Nash was born in Opelousas, Louisiana, on May 23, 1844. At an early age, he moved to New Orleans where he worked as a bricklayer. At nineteen years old, he enlisted in the Tenth Regiment of the Corp d'Afrique at Port Hudson, Louisiana. During a battle at Fort Blakely, Alabama. Sergeant Nash was wounded and he lost his right foot. When he returned to New Orleans, he was appointed night inspector at the Custom House. His political associates there encouraged and supported him to become the Republican candidate for the Sixth Congressional District of Louisiana in 1874, and he was elected to the Forty-fourth Congress of the United States. Unlike his two predecessors, J. Willis Menard and P. B. S. Pinchback, who were both elected to Congress but never seated, Congressman Nash became the first Black man from Louisiana ever seated in Congress. He was assigned to the Committee on Education and Labor. However, it was extremely difficult for him to get anything done in this Democrat-dominated Congress. Congressman Nash served only one term in Congress, losing reelection in 1877.

When he returned to New Orleans, he tried to resume his work as a bricklayer. In 1882, he was appointed postmaster of the Washington Parish Post Office, an appointment which lasted only three months. Because of his war injuries, he was unable to return to laying bricks; he began working as a cigar maker until his death on June 21, 1913. In the past sixteen years, native Louisianians have been elected to Congress representing other states, but since 1877, Louisianians have not elected a Black to represent Louisiana in Congress.

CHARLES PHILLIP ADAMS
EDUCATOR AND FOUNDER OF GRAMBLING STATE UNIVERSITY
JULY 22, 1873-JUNE 27, 1961

Charles P. Adams was born in Brusly, Louisiana, on July 22, 1873. He was the son of ex-slaves and was reared in poverty. He was a dedicated worker, and as a youth, he practiced trading and bartering and thus became prosperous. He and his uncles bought and farmed their own land. He worked his way through Tuskegee Institute and became a devout student of Dr. Booker T. Washington.

In 1901, the North Louisiana Farmer's Relief Association of Ruston, Louisiana, wrote to Dr. Booker T. Washington, president of Tuskegee Institute, asking for a man from Tuskegee to start an industrial school similar in objectives to Tuskegee. On August 4, 1901, Charles P. Adams, a recent graduate of Tuskegee Institute, arrived in Lincoln Parish to start a school in the Allen Green Community.

From these beginnings, this pioneer educator would see the name of this school change several times; he would hear a desperate cry for support and pride in one's accomplishments. Mr. Adams's task was enormous, and he drew from his boyhood experience much in his efforts to build an institution that would train Black people to improve their standards of living through education, agricultural training, and basic skills to earn a living. From 1901 to 1912, this institution was operated from private funds. Through much strife and hardships, Mr. Adams maintained the industrial school concept. In 1918, the school received state support, and in 1928, the school became a junior college. In 1936, Charles P. Adams retired, but his philosophy lives on today on the campus of Grambling State University.

JOSEPH MANUEL BARTHOLOMEW
GOLF-COURSE ARCHITECT/BUSINESS LEADER
AUGUST 1, 1890-OCTOBER 12, 1971

Joseph Manuel Bartholomew, Sr., was born in New Orleans on August 1, 1890. At about the age of seven, while a student in grade school, he worked after school as a caddie at the nearby Audubon Golf Course. He taught himself to play golf, and before long, he became an instructor to older White men. Later, he started working for Audubon Park Club and began running the white-only establishment. In 1922, his keen interest in the game garnered the attention of park officials who sent him to study at the Golf Architectural School in New York. Upon returning to New Orleans, he began designing and building golf courses.

Joe Bartholomew became recognized throughout the country as a designer and builder of golf courses; he started his own construction company and expanded his business into other areas. He also became involved in several successful real-estate investments, an insurance company, and an ice-cream company. He made many contributions to Dillard University and Xavier University, and other charitable and civic organizations in the city of New Orleans.

Joseph Bartholomew died on October 12, 1971, leaving behind monumental golf courses for the public to enjoy. Some of the courses he designed and built are New Orleans Country Club (Metairie), City Park golf courses 1 and 2 (free of charge), and the Joseph M. Bartholomew Memorial Golf Course, named in his honor by the city of New Orleans in 1979. He has been featured in *Sports Illustrated* and *Fortune* magazines for his outstanding contribution to the game of golf and for his business leadership.

MITCHELL PETER LAFRANCE
(GUIDE/DUCK DECOY CARVER)
SEPTEMBER 28, 1882-APRIL 19, 1979

Mitchell Peter Lafrance was born in Point-a-la-hache, Louisiana, on September 28, 1882. His parents died when he was a young boy, and he was raised by Mr. Duplessis, a professional hunting guide and decoy carver. Mr. Duplessis taught him to earn a living by hunting and trapping. In preparing for a hunt, he was taught to build duck blinds, learn duck calls, and to carve working duck decoys out of cypress roots. Mitchell and his nephew, George E. Fredrick, and a friend, Charles N. Jeofrau, would carve decoys for work and their own pleasure. They created a distinct pattern and style of carving and painting decoys, which even today distinguishes their decoys from others. People would buy their decoys not only for duck hunting but to display in their homes as well, where they would be the topic of discussion.

While a young man, Mitchell Lafrance moved to New Orleans, and he worked as a laborer and hod carrier, but he also worked as a guide for some of the wealthiest duck hunters in the South. He was a proud and caring man; he shared his patterns and painting techniques with anyone he could interest in carving. He influenced the works of many contemporary carvers and the folk art of duck carving in the South. When he died at age ninety-six, some people said that Mitchell Lafrance perhaps had carved more ducks than any other Louisiana carver. Mitchell Lafrance, a definitive carver, left a style and pattern that contributed greatly to the art of decoy carving. That art in general and the Louisiana form in particular will forever be indebted to Mitchell Lafrance.

DAVID JULIUS MALARCHER
(PROFESSIONAL BASEBALL MANAGER AND POET)
OCTOBER 18, 1894-MAY 11, 1982

David Julius "Gentleman Dave" Malarcher was born on October 18, 1894, in Whitehall (near Union), Louisiana. He was the youngest of eleven children. He moved to New Orleans where he attended the New Orleans University elementary and college departments. He was player-captain on the New Orleans University baseball team from 1912 through 1916, a period during which the team never lost a game. While still a student, Dave also played semipro baseball for the New Orleans Eagles from 1914 to 1915. He began playing professional baseball for the Indianapolis ABCs until he was inducted into the U.S. Army (where he also played baseball). In 1920, he began his career with the Chicago American Giants. In 1926, Malarcher became third baseman player-manager. He was selected by the then owner-manager Andrew "Rube" Foster, one of the greatest managers in baseball. Malarcher was perhaps the finest third baseman in his day, and he was most respected by his peers and players. In 1926, he led the Chicago American Giants to a pennant victory and the Negro World series in 1926 and 1927, and in 1932, 1933, and 1934. As manager of the Cole's American Giants, he won the league pennants and the world championships. In 1935, he retired from baseball as one of the most successful managers in all of the Negro baseball leagues.

After his retirement from baseball, "Gentleman Dave," as he was affectionately called, began a career as a real estate broker and a poet. His poetry has been published in books, newspapers, and journals. He was keenly aware of the value of education; in memory of his mother, he founded and incorporated the Martha Malarcher Educational Foundation for the educational success of descendants of his family.

PIERRE LANDRY
(POLITICIAN, MINISTER, AND CIVIC LEADER)
1841-1921

Pierre Landry was born on a plantation in Ascension Parish, Louisiana, as a slave but was allowed to live as a free person. He attended a school on the plantation for free children and later was taught a trade of confectioner and cook. At age thirteen, he was sold to the owner of the Houmas Plantation, and at this time, he served as chief pastry man and subsequently as yardman. He was an industrious and ambitious young man. In 1860, he began training as a carpenter. After acquiring his freedom, he moved to Donaldsonville.

From 1868 to 1884, Landry served in a multitude of elected and appointed positions in parish and state government. In 1868, Landry was elected mayor of Donaldsonville, and in the ensuing years, he was elected president of the Ascension Parish Police Jury, member of the school board, and appointed tax collector by the governor. He was elected to both the State House of Representatives, and the Senate before he retired from political life.

Landry was very religious, and as a youngster, he was reared Catholic but later was converted to the Methodist religion. In 1878, he was ordained a deacon and appointed pastor of his church. In 1881, he was appointed presiding elder to the Shreveport District and pastored the St. Paul Church. He became presiding elder of the South New Orleans District in 1891.

In 1873, he became a trustee of New Orleans University, and he also served as principal of Gilbert Academy in 1900.

MARTIN LUTHER KING WALK AND MONUMENT

On August 6, 1976, a three-year project by the city of New Orleans and its residents reached its completion. In an official ceremony, the dedication of a twelve-block walk and a monument to the memory of Dr. Martin Luther King, Jr., the slain civil rights leader of the 1960s, was made official.

The neutral ground (median) of Melpomene Street from Dryades Street to Claiborne Avenue was renamed Martin Luther King Walk. The project consisted of a concrete walkway, landscaping, park benches, game tables, additional lighting, and other improvements to the street. This project was designed by one of the city's finest Black architectural firms, Perkins & James. The center piece of the walk was produced by Southern University's professor Frank Hayden.

Frank Hayden, was born on June 10, 1934, in Memphis, Tennessee. He earned a degree in art at Xavier University. Later, he began his work as a sculptor at Xavier University. He left Xavier to earn a masters of fine arts from Notre Dame University. Hayden traveled to Germany, Denmark, and Sweden to study under other great masters of sculpture. Hayden returned to Louisiana to join the art department at Southern University at Baton Rouge. Hayden was commissioned to produce works for Pope John Paul II, several churches, banks, and governmental buildings throughout this country. He was widely exhibited and has received numerous commissions for architectural sculptures.

The city of New Orleans, commissioned this talented artist to produce a piece of sculpture that would be a fitting tribute to Dr. Martin Luther King, Jr., from the citizens of this city. He created a ten-foot tall cast bronze sculpture. It was cast at the Modern Art Foundry in Long Island, New York, and shipped to New Orleans where it was placed atop a fountain at the entrance to Martin Luther King Walk. This graduate of Xavier University had come back to give something to the city that gave him so much.

Frank Hayden said his piece embodied "Dr. King's lifelong quest for understanding . . . it expresses symbolically people reaching—trying to come together. It represents a simple man of noble ideas."

Inside of the global sphere, surrounded by the outstretched arms, are passages from some of Dr. King's most noted speeches. These words are forever written inside the globe, to leave an indelible message to all—telling us how we are to live for p---- ------ --- - harmony. In 1989, the city council of New Orleans changed the name of M to Martin Luther King Blvd.

FERDINAND LUCIEN ROUSSEVE
(ARCHITECT, EDUCATOR, AND CIVIC LEADER)

Ferdinand Rousseve was born in New Orleans, Louisiana, on July 18, 1904. He received his early education in the private and parochial schools of New Orleans. He earned a bachelor of science degree in architecture from Massachusetts Institute of Technology and a masters in history of art from the University of Chicago. In 1948, he earned a Ph.D. in architecture from Harvard University.

In 1930, Ferdinand Rousseve began teaching architecture and French at Howard University. At one time, he was business manager at Southern University at Baton Rouge for one year. After leaving Southern, he then returned to the classroom again, as an instructor at Xavier University.

In 1933, he became the first Black registered architect in the State of Louisiana. From 1934 to 1948, he was professor and head of the Department of Art at Xavier University. During his tenure as an instructor on the college level, he presented many scholarly papers on subjects in art, architecture, housing and the Catholic Church. Dr. Rousseve was a member of several professional societies.

Ferdinand L. Rousseve was an active civic leader in every community in which he lived: in the New Orleans community and the Cambridge, Massachusetts, community. He was an active influence in the Urban League. In New Orleans, he also served as chairman of the Urban League's board of directors. He served on many committees relative to the Catholic Church and also the city. Dr. Rousseve was active on several interracial justice committees, and he received many certificates and awards for his labors in these capacities.

In 1946, he became a licensed architect in the state of Alabama. In Louisiana, Texas, and Alabama, much of his work as an architect can be found still in use today. Dr. Rousseve was commissioned to draft plans for many buildings; the largest plan of all was for the one-hundred-fifty-bed St. Jude's Catholic Hospital in Montgomery, Alabama. He drew plans for several churches, including St. Augustine's Catholic Church in Klotzville, Central Congregational Church, Rose Hill Baptist Church, Fifth African Baptist Church, all in New Orleans, and several other churches. He was the architect of record for many churches, schools, convents, rectories, parsonages, business establishments, and numerous residences and small apartment buildings. On July 18, 1965, Dr. Rousseve died, leaving behind structures throughout the South that are testimony to this giant among architects and men of the church.

ABRAHAM LINCOLN DAVIS, JR.
(MINISTER, CIVIL RIGHTS LEADER, POLITICIAN)

Abraham Lincoln Davis, Jr., was born in Bayou Goula, Louisiana, on November 2, 1914. He moved to New Orleans as a youngster and was educated in the public schools of Plaquemine and Orleans parishes. He earned a bachelor of arts degree from Leland College. He attended Bible schools in Chicago, Illinois, and New Orleans. As a young man, he became concerned with the conditions of segregation and discrimination in New Orleans. In 1941, he got involved in his first march on the registrar's office to end discrimination against Blacks who wanted to register to vote. In 1943, Rev. Davis was appointed pastor of New Zion Baptist Church. For four decades, Rev. Davis was among the most active and prominent ministers of any denomination in the metropolitan New Orleans area. He guided many religious and civic organizations to serve the people. In 1942, he became active with many religious organizations, including the Ideal Missionary Baptist and Educational Association, Interdenominational Ministerial Alliance, and the Louisiana Baptist State Convention. Many of these organizations he served as the president, chairman, or organizer.

Rev. Davis served the Baptist Church in many areas of education, ministry, outreach, and recruiting. He served unselfishly in many capacities from the Trustee Board of Leland College and Union Baptist Theological Seminary to neighborhood action committees. Rev. Davis was awarded the doctor of divinity degree. His search to serve his people brought him to many distant places. Rev. Davis once served as chairman of the Housing Authority of New Orleans (an agency that governs and regulates public housing for the poor). He was one of the founding board members of Total Community Action and various other city, state, civic, and race relations organizations. In 1949, Dr. Davis was elected the first president of the Orleans Parish Progressive Voters League. Through the OPPVL, many Blacks were taught to register to vote and encouraged to exercise that right.

Dr. Davis was a pioneer in the civil rights movement of the twentieth century. In 1957, a group of ministers and civil rights leaders gathered in the spirit of "We Shall Overcome" to form a nationwide organization to fight racial injustices everywhere through nonviolent direct action. They founded the Southern Christian Leadership Conference. Rev. Martin Luther King, Jr., was elected president, and Dr. A. L. Davis was elected vice president. In 1975, Dr. Davis led one of the first civil rights protest marches in New Orleans. Dr. Davis was one of the key organizers of the march on Washington in 1963.

On the political front, Dr. Davis was one of the founding members of the Orleans Parish Progressive Voters League (OPPVL). When a vacancy occurred on the city council, Dr. Davis was elected unanimously by an all-White city council to become New Orleans's first Black city councilman in the twentieth century. He served on the council for two years. Dr. Abraham Lincoln Davis, Jr., died on June 24, 1978, and was buried in his hometown of Bayou Goula, Louisiana.

GEORGE LONGE
(EDUCATOR, MASONIC AND CIVIC LEADER)

George Longe was born in New Orleans, Louisiana, on July 15, 1898. He was educated in the public schools of New Orleans, Southern University Grammar School, and the College Prep of Straight University. He graduated magna cum laude from Straight University. He studied guidance and counseling and teaching methods at the University of Chicago. Mr. Longe returned to New Orleans and began his career as a classroom teacher at McDonogh 35 High School, the only high school for Black students in New Orleans.

George Longe was affiliated with practically every organization concerned with education or racial equality and community betterment. He distinguished himself as an active participant in organizations throughout the city and state to enhance the quality of education for our children in a less-than-adequate school system.

In 1924, Mr. Longe began his career as a classroom teacher and, in 1929, was promoted to principal. He served as principal of McDonogh 36, Albert Wicker, Macarty, and Alfred Lawless Public Schools. In 1934, Mr. Long developed a course for Negro history for the Orleans Parish public schools. It was accepted and taught in the classrooms. For his work on this course development, he was awarded a certificate of charter membership in Negro Historical Association of Xavier University. Mr. Longe was elected president of the Louisiana Colored Teachers Association. He was the editor of their official journal for twelve years.

In 1921, George Longe joined the L'Amitie Lodge 27 of the Supreme Council of the Ancient & Accepted Scottish Rite of Freemasonry of Louisiana (AASRFM-La.). This organization would remain an intricate part in his daily life. He excelled at what freemasonry could do for his people. In 1925, he reached the top of the freemason ladder when he became a thirty-three degree. Through freemasonry, he found many ways to serve the organization and his community. From 1939 to 1971, he served as the supreme grand commander of the AASRFM-La. Under his leadership, his organization made many outstanding contributions throughout the state of Louisiana.

George Longe's personal commitment to his community broadened the minds of his students and others by encouraging them to give back to society. He was one of the founders of the Greater New Orleans Urban League; chairman of the Negro Division of the War Finance Committee—war-bonds drive in New Orleans; a member of the Bunch Social Club; and many other civic and social organizations. On July 23, 1985, George Longe died at his home in New Orleans.

MILNE BOYS HOME

Alexander Milne, a Scottish-born hardware merchant and slave owner died in 1838. He was very wealthy and was known for his great philanthropy. Milne owned large tracks of land in New Orleans (Gentilly section). Milne's great fortune benefitted many people throughout the world. In New Orleans, he bequeathed that an asylum for destitute orphan boys and another asylum for the relief of destitute orphan girls shall be established at Milneburg. His will was probated on October 23, 1838. His desire to help others was so strong that his entire will was etched on his tomb (located in St. Louis Cemetery #2, Square 2).

Shortly after his death, the construction began on the first of two institutions but was abandoned during the Civil War. The leftovers of these assets were turned over to the city. In 1905, the governor of the state appointed a board of directors to carry out the mandates of the Milne will. The first girls' asylum was located on 295 acres on Bayou St. John and later moved to a location on Gentilly near the current-day Fairgrounds Race Track.

Many years of legal fights were launched in and out of courts between the city, the state, and several human rights groups that were working in the interest of the children. It seems that the money was disappearing and the children were being neglected. When they reached a resolution to the problems, the present-day Milne Asylum for Boys was planned. Construction on the site began in 1929 on the Milne land in the section of New Orleans called Milneburg, at 5400 Franklin Avenue. The first three buildings—an administration building, one dormitory for White boys and one for Black boys—were dedicated and occupied on the same day. The first occupants numbered 146: 42 Whites and 102 Black boys. The White youths came from an orphanage called the Agnew Home, while the Black youths came from the Colored Waifs Home that was located at Conti and City Park Avenue.

The Colored Waifs Home, which had been established in 1901 by Capt. Joseph Jones and his wife, housed Black orphans and juvenile offenders. When Captain Jones returned to New Orleans from the Spanish-American War, he was saddened by the large numbers of destitute Black children on the streets. He sought permission from the city to use a condemned insane asylum to house these destitute children. Capt. Jones housed many homeless children, including those who were found guilty of noncapital offenses. The most noted of the youths committed to the Colored Waifs Home was Louis Armstrong (January 1, 1912).

Today, Milne Boy's Home is a city-operated facility. Youngsters no longer live on the grounds, in spite of the need for more protected shelters and secured learning environments for many wayward Black male youngsters of today. Milne Boy's Home is tied up in controversy once again as the city officials ponder its faith.

ULYSSES GRANT DAILEY
(PHYSICIAN AND EDUCATOR)

Ulysses Grant Dailey was born on August 3, 1885, in Donaldsonville, Louisiana. While growing up in Louisiana, he was greatly influenced by his mother to become a concert pianist and conductor. She taught him to play classical music on the piano. Also, she taught him to be aware of and respectful of the Black leaders of his day.

His family later moved to Fort Worth, Texas, while he was in high school. He was regarded as a bright and gifted student. A local physician who was a professor, in the medical department at Forth Worth University became interested in Ulysses's achievements. In 1902, that physician encouraged him to enter Northwestern Medical School in Chicago, Illinois. He graduated the youngest of fifteen students in his class. Ulysses experienced much discrimination against his race throughout his training, but he still remained focused on becoming a good physician.

From 1908 to 1912, he studied under the world-renowned heart surgeon, Dr. Daniel Hale Williams. Dr. Dailey saw Dr. Williams as his role model as both surgeon and physiologist. He worked as an assistant surgeon to Dr. Williams. Dr. Dailey became a devoted member of the National Medical Association. He later became an associate professor at Providence Hospital. During this time, Dr. Dailey was published in the *New York Medical Journal*.

Dr. Dailey's writing skills were recognized by his professional peers, and he was appointed to the editorial board of the *Journal of the National Medical Association*. He served on that board from 1910 to 1943. In 1914, his surgical skills earned him another great honor. Dr. Dailey's peers elected him chairman of the surgical section of the National Medical Association. One year later, he was elected president of the National Medical Association.

In 1925, Dr. Dailey went to Europe to pursue more knowledge of surgical techniques and also to be relieved from the pressures of working in a highly racist situation. Frustrated by racial barriers and political problems within and outside Providence Hospital, Dr. Dailey decided to open his own hospital, freeing himself from the politics and policies and philosophy that caused him much grief. He purchased two stone houses on the corner of Thirty-seventh Street and Michigan Ave. in Chicago, Illinois. After remodeling the houses, he named them the Dailey Hospital and Sanitarium. Dr. Dailey was the hospital's surgeon-in-chief for six years. He was a frequent lecturer at Northwestern University and Surgeon Emeritus at Providence Hospital. He cofounded the International College of Surgeons. Dr. Dailey became one of the first four Black members of the American College of Surgeons. He served as associate editor of the *Journal of the National Medical Association* for thirty-eight years. Dr. Ulysses Grant Dailey died in Chicago, Illinois on April 22, 1961.

AUTOCRAT SOCIAL & PLEASURE CLUB

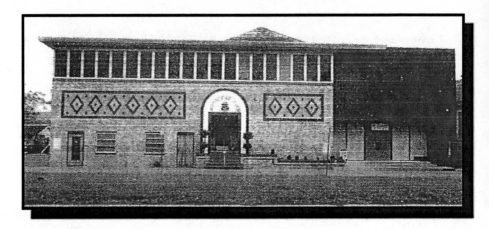

The year was 1909, and for Black men standing on a street corner in New Orleans, this meant possible harassment from police. These were the circumstances that brought twelve Black men together to talk of an alternative to standing on these corners. They wanted a place to entertain themselves in peace. Simon Belleu, a member of the group, acquired a charter for a poker club, and this charter provided protection for him and his friends, where they could congregate and play poker or other games, safe from the harassment of the police. However, this group did not last very long. One gentleman, Arthur Boisdore, from that group decided to continue that style of entertainment. He secured the charter from Simon Belleu to continue the club under the name the Autocrat Club.

This first group operated on St. Philip and Claiborne streets. This Autocrat Club was a closed corporation, and the profits from their operations were divided between them. Their operation lasted a short time. Later, in the summer of 1914, another group of Black men came together to recreate and play card games. Among this group were Arthur Boisdore, Placide Suane, Louis Smith, Gabe Pratts, Walter and Wallace Marine, and Edward Labuzan. Arthur Boisdore served briefly as its first president, and Edward Labuzan followed during that first year. The members enjoyed each other's company so much that they began discussing plans for a permanent safe haven to entertain themselves without interferences from the police.

On September 14, 1914, the membership voted to continue to operate under the charter of the Autocrat Club. Ten men put up one dollar each; they elected officers to run the club, and they rented a two-room house on Onzaga Street from which to operate.

The Autocrat members realized a need to make the games profitable so that they could provide the club with operating funds. During the next few months, the young Autocrat members were faced with discrimination from its White neighbors as they didn't want the club as neighbors. The club moved a couple of times before renting a house on St. Bernard near Claiborne Ave., which is the current home of the club.

Several men requested membership into the club. The membership grew quickly, making it necessary for the club to meet twice a month just to consider new members. Soon the members had to look at the club as a business. The president appointed a committee to determine ways and means of maintaining its operation. Recognizing itself on a solid base, the club purchased the Autocrat charter from Belleu and Boisdore for thirty dollars. A committee was formed to draft a constitution and bylaws, and at a regular meeting, the members adopted its constitution, bylaws, and a new name—the Autocrat Social & Pleasure Club.

According to its constitution, the club is to "promote social intercourse, harmony, enjoyment, refinement of manners, and the moral, mental and material welfare of its members." The membership worked to enhance its community through its cultural and intellectual enrichment of its membership. During these formative years, the club struggled to develop its own philosophy and ideology as a group. They established a library complete with a variety of intellectual reading materials and a large collection of "Negro history" materials. They engaged in social and sporting activities and a symphony orchestra for the benefit of its membership. Their membership included a cross section of men from the metropolitan New Orleans area, from various occupations and backgrounds. In 1924, the club acquired its present location (1725 St. Bernard Ave.).

The Autocrat Club has been a major sponsor of athletic competitions in the club and in outside leagues. These activities included baseball, basketball, tennis, and golf. In 1934, a newsletter, the *Autocrat Voice*, was created to inform their membership of what their club and its membership were doing. The Autocrat's auditorium has been more than a landmark in the Seventh Ward; it has served this community as a hub for civic and political issues and civil rights meetings during the 1960s, as well as a site for social entertainment and cultural growth.

DRYADES STREET LIBRARY

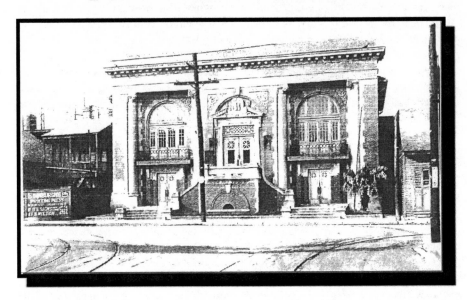

During the days of segregation in the South, public libraries were not available to everyone. White people and Black attorneys were allowed to use the public libraries in New Orleans. However, the Blacks attorneys were confined to read or research the law books only. A great need existed among Blacks in New Orleans to use the books in the public library. During the early 1900s, local Black leaders demanded that the library board provide a branch library for Black citizens. An educator, James H. Dillard, for who Dillard University is named, was instrumental in getting the Andrew Carnegie Foundation to pledge money for construction of a library for Blacks. The city donated the site for the building, and the Andrew Carnegie Foundation kept their promise and donated the money to construct the building and furnish it. It costed $25,000 to construct, and it had a capacity for ten thousand volumes. Besides the books, it had meeting rooms that the Black civic groups were invited to use.

The Dryades Street Public Library Branch opened on October 23, 1915. It was a day of jubilation in New Orleans among Blacks. At the dedication ceremony, Black leaders representing the various segments of the city were allowed to express their gratitude for having a library branch opened to the Black citizens. The range of speakers at the ceremony included the Black physicians, lawyers, public school teachers, and civic leaders. At the dedication ceremony J. Madison Vance, a physician and strong advocate for the library branch, said, "The Black community is indeed grateful and pleased to have the newest and largest branch library; however, I regret there is not more books on the shelves written by Black authors."

However, the meeting rooms on the ground floor were used by many of the civic groups. The Dryades Street YMCA, the Negro Board of Trade, the Colored Young Men's Business Association, the National Association for the Advancement of Colored People (NAACP), the Negro History and Study Club, and many others made used of this facility. This building was the showplace of the Black community. When nationally known Blacks would visit the city, this library branch would be included on the list of places to visit.

The Dryades Street Public Library became the hub of learning activities for school children. In 1939, a "satellite" location was established in St. Peter Claver's School. The library spawned reading clubs throughout the city. Most notable of this branch's services were the satellites that were located in the housing projects. Each of the housing projects had its own reading or book club for the children and the adults.

The Dryades Street Public Library Branch remained a segregated branch until 1955, when the entire library system was desegregated. The use of this building as a library ended in 1965 after severe damage by Hurricane Betsy. Shortly after the hurricane, a fire badly damaged the building, leaving it too costly for the city to repair, so it was closed. For the next quarter of a century, this building was occupied to be a motel for a short time, but it remained vacant for many years.

The Dryades Street Branch Public Library played was an indispensable role in the educational, economic, and social development of the Black community. Then, the Dryades Street Young Men's Christian Association (YMCA) purchased the building to expand its community programs. A strong effort to revitalize the once-commanding presence this building played in uptown New Orleans has been underway for some time. The latest plans to renovate the building for use as a pre-kindergarten day care and employment training and development for citizens in need of the job training services.

MADAME C. J. WALKER
BUSINESS PIONEER AND PHILANTHROPIST

On December 23, 1867, Sarah Breedlove was born in Delta, Louisiana. Both her parents were ex-slaves and poor. Reared on a farm, she was orphaned at age seven and left under the care of a sister. She married at age fourteen and became a widow at twenty, with one small daughter. Sarah Breedlove McWilliams, industrious and eager to get ahead, moved to several states to find work, accepting odd jobs wherever she went.

Sarah was not particularly pleased with her personal appearance, especially her hair and skin. She began to experiment on her own uncultivated hair and skin. After many trials and failures, she developed her secret formula to soften her hair and give it a glossy natural look. Her neighbors noticed the change in her hair and they begged for portions of her hair and scalp ointment for their use. In 1900, she started selling her products, and soon, Sarah McWilliams was into the hair-products business. She developed many hair-care products, and for the first time in America, Negro men and women were able to groom their hair and skin with products developed specifically for them.

In 1906, she married Charles J. Walker, a newspaper man. In 1912, they divorced, but she kept his name, preferring to be called Madame C. J. Walker. She continued developing new products and opened beauty schools across the country. She moved to Denver, Colorado, and established a mail-order service and appointed regional agents to sell her products. Her enterprising business afforded many Blacks throughout the country to get involved in their own business as sales persons and/or hairdressers. Madame C. J. Walker became the first Negro woman in the U.S. to become a millionaire by her own success as a cosmetologist.

Madame Walker was a financial success, and she shared her wealth with needy people through humanitarian organizations purchasing food and clothing and supporting Black Institutions of higher learning. Her philanthropy earned her nationwide attention in life and death. Even today, a large portion of the company profits are given to educational institutions and charitable organizations. Madame Walker and her daughter were great supporters of the artists and artisans of the Harlem Renaissance (Black Renaissance). They became supporters of most any movement that would aid Black people.

Economy Hall

The Societé Economier et d'Assistance Mutuelle (The Society of the Economy and Mutual Aid Association) of New Orleans was founded on March 1, 1836. The opening paragraph of their preamble reads "Benevolence, that sentiment so pure and noble, being a celestial emanation, is the fundamental basis of this Association." For more than one and a quarter centuries, the preamble of this organization gave many examples of its benevolence to its members and the community. Its purpose was to provide for the maintenance of the association; to assist its sick members by providing a physician and medicine in time of need; and provide for the funeral and burial of their deceased members; perform charitable and benevolent act for the less fortunate throughout the community. This organization played an important role in the growth and development of the community. Its meeting hall leaves an indelible mark on history. In many areas such as religion, music, human rights, and the development of many benevolent citizens.

In September 1856, the society purchased an old building at 1422 Ursuline Street, in the Tremé section of New Orleans. They demolished the building, and on the lot, they built a two story, multipurpose meeting hall and living quarters for a caretaker. The society rented the meeting hall to many community organizations for their public and private events. Several benevolent and mutual-aid societies were organized here and held their meetings and social and fundraising events here. Many notable organizations used this hall as a site for meetings and fundraising events.

During the Reconstruction era, the state legislature enacted laws, which discriminated against Black citizens. On September 5, 1891, eighteen Black civic and community leaders organized themselves into the citizens' committee at the Economy Hall. Their purpose was to wage a legal battle against these state statues that discriminated against Black people. The committee challenged Act 111 of the 1886 Louisiana Legislature, which forbade the mixing of races in common carriers traveling from one state to another and from one place to another within the state. The committee challenged through the newspapers and in the courts. Its most noted battle was *Plessey v. Ferguson*. Homer Plessey acting for the citizens' committee was arrested for riding in the White section of a train. The committee filed a lawsuit, which was defeated in the local courts, so the committee filed a federal suit. Their case was argued before the United States Supreme Court. The high court ruled against Homer Plessy and the committee when the court established the doctrine of "separate but equal." This landmark ruling resulted in all municipalities throughout the country displaying "Colored only and White only" signs in all public places of accommodation, and Homer Plessy was fined $25.00 for violating the law.

During the early 1900s many organizations such as the Bulls, the San Jacinto, the Iroquois clubs and many others would host dances and jazz concerts here. More than twenty benevolent societies at one time or another called this hall home. The first floor of the building was used by many community, civic, and social organizations for holding their meetings and other events. For the musicians who played here, it was considered the premiere hall in Black New Orleans to play. To the young aspiring musicians, one could come here to see and listen to the best in the pioneers of New Orleans jazz anywhere in the country. Among the long list of jazz pioneers and popular bands to perform here were George Lewis, Manuel Perez's Imperial Band, Bunk Johnson, Freddie Keppard's Creole Band, Kid Ory, Johnny and Baby Dodds, Alphonse Picou, Sidney Bechet, and the ambassador of jazz, Louis Armstrong.

As the 1940s approached, the demand for the use of the hall ceased, and so, on November 3, 1945, the society rented their building to the St. Mark Missionary Baptist Church. In August of 1965, Hurricane Betsy devastated the city of New Orleans and Economy Hall was damaged beyond repair. St. Mark Missionary Baptist Church was ordered to abandon the building, and they moved to 1501 Ursuline Street. The city ordered the Economy Hall to be demolished. One hundred six years of service to the New Orleans community came to an end.

SAINT AUGUSTINE
ROMAN CATHOLIC CHURCH

In 1724, the Roman Catholic Church established itself as the only church of the Louisiana Territory. It extended its arms to evangelize the slaves and native Indians of the territory in a document called the Black Code. This code mandated that slave owners provide means for slaves to practice the Catholic faith. For many slaves and free people of color, this strange and distant religion offered protection, faith, and hope, along with a newfound awareness of Christianity.

In 1825, a French woman, Marie Aliquot, vowed to devote her life to help Blacks and slaves receive instructions. She purchased a square of land bound by Ursuline, Liberty, Gov. Nicholls and St. Claude streets, where she established the first school for free Black children. In 1836, the Ursuline nuns bought the property with the condition that they continue to educate Black children. They did until 1838. In this period, most of the people living outside the old city (Vieux Carré) attended Mass in the small St. Claude Street Chapel, which adjoined the school for Black children. The quarters were small, and as the congregation grew, a larger church was needed. The Ursuline nuns donated the land for the erection of a church with the provision that the archdiocese name it in honor of their patron Saint Augustine.

In 1841, the construction of the church began on the corner of Gov. Nicholls and Saint Claude streets and was completed in September of 1842. St. Augustine became the fourth Roman Catholic parish to be established in New Orleans. The first pastor, Father Rousselon, was responsible for the formation of the Sisters of the Holy Family, the only predominantly Black order of nuns in the United States. St. Augustine Church served the faithful who lived outside of the old city and those who lived in the Tremé section of New Orleans.

There has been some controversy as to who funded the building of the church. Some authorities asserted that some Catholic priests went out into the community collecting contributions from the Black refugees from Haiti, the free people of color, and Creoles of the area. It is known, however, that the bishop of Louisiana contributed the majority of the money needed for the construction.

From the beginning, this church was considered the church of the free people of color and Creoles of the area. The annual pew-rental records indicate that half the pews were rented to Blacks. The pews to the side of the main aisles were designed specifically for use by slaves.

Over the years, St. Augustine has been the site of many historic events, including the ordination of the Sisters of the Holy Family which occurred on November 21, 1842. Noteworthy figures who have worshiped here include Maurice Rousseve, one of the first Black priests from Louisiana in the twentieth century, and Alexander P. Tureaud, the prominent civil rights attorney who was baptized at St. Augustine. Most recently, Rev. Curtis J. Guillory, SVD, who was first Black pastor (1976-1982) was ordained the twelfth Black bishop in the U.S. in 1988.

STRAIGHT UNIVERSITY

The end of the Civil War and the prohibition of slavery brought to the South more than a decade of Congressional reconstruction. To implement this, the South was divided into five military districts. The federal occupation troops were given the charge of enforcing the Fourteenth Amendment (granted citizenship to all born or naturalized U.S. citizens) to the U.S. Constitution and the new statutes related to Negro suffrage. One of their responsibilities was to establish systems of public education. To support this, the first school tax was levied on the states to fund education. Only three southern states, Louisiana included, attempted to launch schools on a nonsegregated basis.

In 1868, the Louisiana Constitutional Convention placed a ban on segregated schools in Louisiana. In New Orleans, the Orleans Parish School Board opposed the law, and they challenged it in the courts, who declared it legal. However, there were few desegregated public schools, but this ushered in numerous segregated schools for Whites. However, with the help of the Freedmen Bureau and the American Missionary Association (AMA) a very important school was established for Black students.

On June 25, 1869, the American Missionary Association chartered Straight University and established a board of directors. They purchased the land located at Esplanade and Derbigny streets and the Freedmen's Bureau erected the building, and Mr. Seymore Straight, a benefactor and Baptist educator, donated operating capital, for this and the school was named in his honor. By February 1870, Straight opened its doors for the first time. They established a normal department with special emphasis to train school teachers. On June 9, 1876, the first-class graduate from the normal department. It consisted of two women and eight men.

After just seven years of operation on the corner of Esplanade and Derbigny streets, an arsonist burned the building to the ground. Before tragedy struck, more than four thousand students had attended class at Straight. Classes were then convened in Central Church, later to be renamed Central Congregational Church. In 1878, classes resumed at the new campus on Canal and Tonti streets when the first building, Straight Hall, was opened.

In 1908, the AMA reclassified Straight University as a secondary school after closing the theology department. Under President E. M. Stevens, Straight school was renamed Straight College. It continued its teacher-training program. He also initiated a football program and phased out the primary and secondary grades. In 1915, the board of trustees changed the name from Straight University to Straight College.

SISTERS OF THE HOLY FAMILY

The Sisters of the Holy Family, the first community of Black Catholic nuns organized in the South and the second in the United States, had their humble beginnings in New Orleans, Louisiana, on November 21, 1842. Under the leadership of the founder, Henriette Delille, these young women wanted a ministry of total dedication in a religious life to charity, the ignorant, the poor, the orphans and the sick of this community. And so, upon recognition into the church as a legal organization, they were trained and educated in the proper doctrines and procedures of religious life in the Roman Catholic Church.

Father Etienne Rousselon, the pastor of the newly constructed St. Augustine's church, rented a small house on St. Bernard Street for the sisters to use as a convent and center from which to work. On that same day, they began their work by taking in two old ladies. On July 11, 1847, Henriette Delille, with help of the free men of color of the community, they organized the Association of the Holy Family for the purpose of incorporating the St. Bernard Home for the Aged and to provide for the relief of the poor and sick people. This incorporation became the first Catholic home for the aged in the United States. The sisters worked day and night to feed and care for the sick and indigents in their charge. They often ran out of food and money, so they turned to the community by begging for donations and assistance from anyone who would listen to them.

On August 15, 1848, with the help of the association, the sisters purchased the property on St. Bernard Avenue. Mother Henriette Delille later purchased the property at No. 172 Hospital Street, which was used as a convent and hospice house for some elderly indigent ladies and willed it, at her death, to her community.

On October 15, 1852, Henriette Delille, Josephine Charles, and Juliette Gaudin took their first vows of the Catholic Church towards becoming nuns. Henriette was formally named the superior and the mistress of novices. Their community grew in numbers, and their services to the less fortunate increased. They established a school for orphaned children, which at the time was against the law.

On November 16, 1862, Mother Henriette Delille died and was buried in a tomb which she had purchased in St. Louis Cemetery # 2, where today many of her sisters in Christ are also entombed. She had changed the lifestyle of her people in their civic, home, and spiritual development. Her spirit lives on in her sisters and in her people.

On August 23, 1870, Mother Josephine Charles purchased a piece of property at 348 Chartres Street for an orphanage and their first normal school. In 1873, the sisters began missionary work outside of New Orleans. They began teaching at an elementary school in Opelousas, Louisiana.

On July 27, 1881, the sisters exchanged the Chartres Street property and several vacant lots for one piece of property located at 717 Orleans Street. Here they established their motherhouse and novitiate and St. Mary's Academy (pictured above), the first secondary school for Black girls in New Orleans. In need of more space for the orphan children, the sisters built an orphanage for children on the same square, and they called it St. John Berchman. Mr. Thomy Lafon, a great Black philanthropist, came to their aid and built them a chapel, a new home for the aged and infirmed on the corner of Tonti and Gov. Nicholls streets. He also built for the sisters a boys and girls orphanage. This facility was named in his honor, Thomy Lafon Old Folks Home.

The sisters struggled with poverty and hardships every day to keep their ministry alive. In 1905, the sisters purchased one hundred and twenty acres of land in the Gentilly section of New Orleans, where they established the Thomy Lafon Boys Home, the current motherhouse and novitiate, the new Lafon Nursing Home, the Delille Manor Senior Citizens Home, and St. Mary's Academy (all-girls high school) are all operated by the Sisters of the Holy Family. The sisters would later allow the Archdiocese of New Orleans to build St. Paul the Apostle Catholic Church on their land.

In 1988, The Sisters of the Holy Family were informed by the Vatican that they may proceed with the cause of canonization of Mother Henriette Delille. This is the beginning of the process by which a person is elevated to be named a saint. Mother Henriette Delille could well be the first Black North American to become a saint in the Roman Catholic Church.

ST. JAMES CHAPEL AFRICAN METHODIST EPISCOPAL CHURCH

In 1844, when slavery in Louisiana was sanctioned by the law and a large segment of the Black population was enslaved, a small group of free people of color, inspired by Rev. Jordan W. Early, an African Methodist Episcopal minister, established their own church. The group, members of St. Paul Methodist Episcopal Church (now Wesley Methodist Church), reached their decision because that church had a mixed congregation, including Whites, free people of color, and slaves. Whites worshiped on the ground floor, while the very small balcony or gallery was set aside for slaves and free people of color.

The group of ten led by a blacksmith, Charles Doughty, rented a site on the corner of Villere and Bienville streets and held services there, calling themselves the African Methodist Episcopal Church. Almost immediately, the congregation was annoyed by the police, who objected to their allowing slaves to attend services because they feared that the new congregation would incite slaves to seek freedom. But the leaders persevered and their faith community increased. Soon their quarters became too small, and they sought land to build their church.

On October 6, 1848, the state issued a charter to the African Methodist Episcopal Church authorizing it to legally operate in Louisiana, with ten founders as incorporators. Charles Doughty was elected president of the board of trustees. According to the charter, slaves were not allowed to become members of the church or the corporation. By December of 1848, the board had purchased a site for the new church in the suburb of Tremé. The entire congregation carried materials to the site where the church was being built. They named the new church St. James Chapel African Methodist Episcopal Church and affiliated with the AME Church of the United States of America.

The new church's first pastor was Rev. John M. Brown, a northerner. He encountered much hostility because he allowed slaves to attend the services. Under the leadership of Rev. Brown, the church grew both in membership and financial stability. As the organizers of the first AME church in New Orleans, the board actively helped to organize and build other AME churches in the area.

From 1858 to 1862 St. James Chapel was closed by the police because its members advocated an end to slavery. During the Civil War, a company of Black Union soldiers was organized by Colonel James Lewis, and they used the church as their headquarters. In 1865, St. James Chapel sponsored the first AME Louisiana conference meeting in New Orleans. St. James Chapel AME Church is still growing and praising the Lord.

Pythian Temple

The Grand Lodge, colored order of the Knights of Pythias of Louisiana, was established in 1880. Like most fraternal organizations of this, they provided health and death insurance and many other benefits to its membership. From their beginnings in Louisiana, the organization struggled with many challenges to achieve greatness unlike that of most fraternal organizations. When the state lodge elected Smith W. Green, Grand Master of Finance, the organization began to rid itself of some of it financial burdens associated with growth.

In 1908, Mr. Green, an insurance executive, had also become the international supreme chancellor of the colored order of the Knights of Pythias of the world, proposed constructing a temple of its own to house all of its organization's operation. The organization approved his plan, and they proceeded to purchase two lots in downtown New Orleans, upon which construction of the building followed. This was the biggest financial venture into a building of its kind ever attempted to date by a Black organization in the United States. The temple is situated on the downtown river corner of Gravier and Saratoga streets, it measures 110 feet deep, 64 feet wide and 102 feet high, in the central business district of New Orleans.

On August 18, 1909, the building was completed and formally dedicated (see above). The total cost of construction was two hundred and one thousand dollars ($ 201,000). They held a four-day grand dedication service, which included, among other things, a parade, church services, and a musical program. When the building opened its doors for business, it became the showpiece of the Black people throughout the South, and it played an important role in supporting the local community in many ways. The facilities of the building included offices and lodge rooms, a barber shop, a theater, facilities for a bank, and all of the modern conveniences of its day. The second floor was occupied by an opera house and an auditorium. The facility was designed with business and entertainment in mind.

Some of the Black businesses who moved their business operation into the Pythian Temple building included their own insurance company, the Industrial Life Insurance Company of Louisiana; the Peoples Benevolent Industrial Life Insurance Company of Louisiana, which was headed by Walter L. Cohen, a prominent political leader of this day; and the Negro Board of Trade had its offices in the Pythian Temple also.

In 1925, two prominent New Orleanians, C. C. Dejoie, Sr., and O. C. W. Taylor established a company here, and they published the *New Orleans Herald-Louisiana Weekly* newspaper. They later renamed the newspaper *The Louisiana Weekly* newspaper, and it has since moved to other quarters, but it is still published today.

In the 1930s, some of its facilities were used as temporary quarters for medical clinics for the patients of Charity Hospital, during the time that the current facility was under construction. In 1909, the temple's theater became the catalyst for the Zulu Social Pleasure and Aid Club. At that time a musical comedy entitled *The Smart Set* was performed in their theatre by an all-Black cast. Among the skits performed was one depicting a powerful African king of a Zulu tribe who boasted, "There never was and there will be another king like me!" After the show, John L. Metoyer and a group of men who were sitting in the audience organized themselves into a club that would come together in costume on Mardi Gras Day to masquerade and mock Rex, the so-called King of New Orleans Mardi Gras. They decided to parade throughout the city on Mardi Gras Day to have fun as the Zulu Club.

Under Chancellor Green, the international colored order of the Knights of Pythias' investments would grow to the millions of dollars. This organization amassed some of the most valuable and most impressive real estate of any Black organization in the country. Including a hot-spring water resort located at Hot Springs, Arkansas. In October of 1925, Supreme Chancellor Green, in a statement of progress of the Knights of Pythias, boasted of a membership of 294,222 and more than $8 million-dollar assets. In Louisiana, they had a total asset of $507,564 and a membership of 8,910, with a maximum of insurance in force amounting to $4,455,000. But when the organization came upon hard times and went into bankruptcy, a U.S. district court valued the building at $325,000. However, in 1941, outstanding taxes and a poor economy caused the Knights of Pythias to lose the building.

San Jacinto Social and Pleasure Club

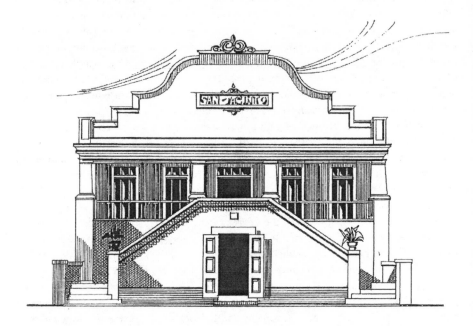

During the summer of 1901, in a small, stuffy backroom of Baptiste's blacksmith shop on Carondelet Walk, between Marais and North Villere streets, in the Tremé section of New Orleans, a group of Black men met daily to play cards. They used a simple table and horseshoe nail kegs for chairs. This provided the setting for a group of men, who found recreation, friendship, and comfort in their gatherings. They agreed on some simple rules: the losers would buy beer, cigarettes, soft drinks, and candles by which to see. They also agreed that after ample refreshments and candles were purchased, the excess monies would remain in the pot, which soon grew into an attractive sum of money. They finally decided to form a club and to rent a house of their own to play cards.

Bill Callioux, one of the players, posted a sign at the entrance to the blacksmith shop, asking anyone who would like to become a member of their club to please sign their name on the sheet of paper and place ten cents opposite their names. A month later, twenty-five men had signed up to become members of this new club. This group organized a club to continue what they were doing. As the membership grew, they decided to move into larger and more permanent quarters. They rented a house on St. Peter near Villere Street, and each member donated furnishings for the house. The house was riddled with large rat holes, and so, at its first membership meeting, they voted to name the club the Rat Hole Club.

The newly formed Rat Hole Club held its first fundraiser around Thanksgiving Day, which grew to become an annual event. The club grew in numbers, and soon, they had to seek larger quarters to accommodate its membership. They stayed in the same neighborhood, but they moved several times to accommodate their growing membership. In 1903, the club joined a baseball league with five other social and pleasure clubs. By August of 1903, the membership had grown to more than two hundred, and the name was changed to the San Jacinto Social and Pleasure Club.

The membership was determined to stay together and grow. They provided many social and athletic activities for its members and the community in general. In addition to playing cards, they organized a precision-drill team which would compete against other Black clubs, a reading room with a supply of the latest books about Black people written by Black authors, a pool table, and a twenty-piece orchestra was organized among its membership by T. V. Baquet. The orchestra enhanced the club's popularity.

The club had its ups and downs: they suffered through financial problems, their membership dropped below one hundred, and the club came close to being evicted because they couldn't pay their rent. In May of 1907, they sponsored a dance at the Economy Hall on Ursuline Street. It was so successful that they were able to resolve their financial problems and their membership increased to more than two hundred members once again. In 1915, the club purchased a piece of property at 1422 Dumaine Street for $ 3,500 on credit. The club beamed with joy as they prospered once again. The club provided many benefits to their membership, including a sick benefit of $ 2.00 a week to members who became incapacitated; when a member died, each member was assessed twenty five cents and the proceeds were turned over to the widow of the family. Every member was obligated to pay his poll tax each and every year, otherwise that person would be expelled from the club if he could not vote.

The club became so popular in the community that their membership catapulted to more than eight hundred members. This brought on another problem of space and accommodations. In 1922, the membership voted to demolish the old building and construct a new and larger facility. On Sunday, September 3, 1922, the orange and gold colors of the new San Jacinto Social and Pleasure Club building was formally blessed and dedicated (see above). Their new $25,000 home at 1422 Dumaine Street was one of the finest facilities in the city belonging to a Black social and pleasure club. Their dedication unveiled to the community a model of harmony and determination, which the membership provided for their community as a showpiece of Black unity and courage. For the next forty-seven years, this structure was host to many benevolent aid societies, musical events, including jazz, honky-tonk, rhythm-and-blues musicians, amateur boxing, and many Mardi Gras Day masqueraders and other cultural events indigenous to the Tremé community.

In the 1960s, the city administration decided to construct a cultural center, and so the building was destroyed by the city to make way for a parking lot. The city later used all of the property on this square for the Armstrong Park.

Xavier University

Southern University was established as an institution of higher learning in 1881. It conducted classes in New Orleans from its beginning to 1915. However, when Southern University closed its doors in New Orleans, it indirectly spawned the seeds for Xavier University. When the state ordered Southern University to move to Scotlandville, Louisiana, the Black Catholics of New Orleans voiced their opposition to the move. Because a large segment of Southern's student population were Roman Catholics. During this time in New Orleans, all of the other institutions of higher learning were established and administered by either the Baptist, Methodist, or Congregational churches.

These non-Catholic schools trained their students for the ministry in their denomination, when the dominant religion among Blacks in New Orleans was Catholic. The Catholic Church was gravely aware of the large number of Black Catholics they were losing to the other denominations because of their schools. When it became certain that Southern University would be relocating to Scotlandville, Louisiana, a group of Black Catholics, led by Medard H. Nelson, an educator and devout Catholic, petitioned the archbishop of the Catholic Church of New Orleans to provide an institution of higher learning for Black Catholics living in New Orleans. The archbishop called upon Mother Katherine Drexel, the founder and superior of a community of nuns—the Sisters of the Blessed Sacrament for Negroes and Indians. They were asked to come to New Orleans and establish a school of higher learning for Black Catholic.

In 1915, Reverend Mother Katherin Drexel arrived in New Orleans to establish a school. She purchased the old Southern University site at 5116 Magazine Street, in the name of the sisters. They used books and materials left over by Southern University to established a normal school with special emphasis on a Catholic education. When the sisters moved into the old Southern University building, they had "Xavier" cut into the stone above the front entrance. On September 21, 1915, the school was formerly opened, and it was named in honor of St. Francis Xavier, a sixth-century priest and scholar.

In 1918, the State Department of Education granted the school a charter to establish a two-year normal school. The school grew very quickly and soon experienced overcrowding. In 1921, the sisters help to find jobs for their graduates; many became teachers in the normal schools, one of only a few professional jobs open to Blacks at that time. In 1925, the sisters were granted state approval to confer a four-year degree and grant diplomas. It established a teachers training college and the liberal arts college with forty-seven students, and they conferred their first college degree on June 6, 1928. The next few years saw much progress, such as establishment of the premedical, pharmacy, and social services departments. The campus grew in size, with several buildings and a stadium and intercollegiate athletics added.

In 1932, the sisters moved into the university into a new facility with two hundred eighty-seven students. It was situated at Plametto and Pine streets. The campus began with three school buildings, designed in an adaptation of the English gothic pattern and were built of Indiana limestone. A preparatory school was established on the Magazine Street site. By the end of the 1936 school year, 2,364 students from twenty states had completed their training and had earned a degree from Xavier University.

To date, Xavier University has played a tremendous role in forging education in the Black people throughout the country. It is governed by a biracial board of trustees and a Black male president; and the Sisters of the Blessed Sacrament continues to maintain a vital presence in administrative and teaching assignments on the campus. Xavier University has bestowed thousands of academic degrees upon its graduates, and it prepares many students for entrance into many professional and graduate schools. It has the distinction of being the only Catholic university in the United States established for Black people, and it has one of the largest pharmacy schools in the country.

LELAND COLLEGE

During Reconstruction in Louisiana, when the masses of Blacks were enslaved, Louisiana's laws provide for no education or religious training for the slaves and poor Blacks. As the federal troops moved into the South to help establish schools for Blacks, they joined with northern evangelist from the Baptist and Methodist churches who came into the South to assist the Black people in acquiring the basic facilities and personnel to establish educational institutions.

In 1870, the American Baptist Home Mission Society (ABHMS) felt a strong need to train ministers of the gospel and teachers for the schools. In the basement of the Tulane Avenue Baptist Church, a group of missionaries organized Leland College and established a board of directors. Its purpose was "to prepare ministers and teachers and to qualify men for business."

The ABHMS and the Baptist Free Mission Society both gave $ 12,500.00 each to purchase ten acres of land fronting on St. Charles Avenue at Wall Street. A deacon and member of the board of directors of the ABHMS, Holbrook Chamberlain, donated the money to build the first building. He had also donated the land upon which to build the First Free Mission Baptist Church, predecessor of the first location of the Tulane Avenue Baptist Church. The board of directors named the school in honor of his wife, Mrs. Lela Chamberlain. The federal government, through the Freedmen's Aid Bureau, also gave $ 17,000.00 towards the erection of a building. In 1871, the school was opened to all without distinction of color, sex, or religion.

In the beginning, the school was a primary grade school, but it soon advanced to a grammar and to a high school, and finally to a university level. It accomplished its goal in providing a quality education to poor people. By 1876, Leland had included theology and science departments to its academic program. Tuition was free to theology students and all others paid a minimal fee. The American Baptist Home Mission Society contributed annually to the operating expense of the school. The state of Louisiana also contributed to its operating budget. Through the society and Leland College, several feeder schools from cities in close proximity to New Orleans were established to support their enrollment. The graduates of Leland often became teachers at the feeder schools.

In 1915, a hurricane severely damaged the buildings and the board of directors decided it would be too costly to repair. They then decided to relocate outside of New Orleans to be more centrally located in the state. They sold the New Orleans property, and, in 1917, they purchased a farm near Alexandria, Louisiana, for the new school, but because of objections from White people living in the area, that site was abandoned. The board then purchased a two-hundred-thirty-six acre farm in Baker, Louisiana. They used thirty-five acres for their new campus. Eight years later, Leland College reopened its doors in Baker, Louisiana, approximately ten miles north of Baton Rouge, as a Christian school.

In 1923, Leland College grew with a strong philosophy, and they established programs and opportunities for their students to develop their mental, spiritual, and physical needs with sports programs and emphasis on academics. They welcomed students of any denomination. The main buildings on this new campus were the Chamberlain Hall, a men's dormitory and women's dormitory (which accommodated two hundred students), a convention hall, the president's house, and a facility cottage. By 1942, the student population had grown to 1,135, which included extension and ministry students, who came from more than eight states. This fine institution soon experienced some difficulties meeting their financial obligations. It was determined that the school should be closed, and in 1959, the last class graduated from Leland College.

SOUTHERN UNIVERSITY

Southern University was established in New Orleans by an act-of-the-state-legislature meeting at New Orleans in January 1881. This act was the result of an article approved by the state constitutional convention of 1867 which was sponsored and promoted by three Black delegates: P. B. S. Pinchback, T. T. Allain, and Henry Dumas. The local community was mixed on the establishment of a university for the Black citizens of the state. Some Black opponents felt that the establishment of a predominantly Black institution of higher learning would segregate the Black community and could be a cause for inferior educational support from the state. Yet others felt that there was no need for an institution for Blacks. Amidst much controversy and dissention throughout the state, which would cross racial and religious lines, Southern University was established by the state legislature.

On March 3, 1881, an act of incorporation was filed in New Orleans and signed by twelve incorporators who also acted as the first board of trustees of Southern University. With an appropriation from the state, they established classes at an old school located at 158 Calliope Street. When the school opened its doors for the first time, twelve students were enrolled. As the enrollment quickly grew, the board determined that this facility was too small, so it began planning for a larger school. It was closed for a brief period, from July 1881 to October 1882.

On August 15, 1885, the board purchased a block of land in Jefferson City, which would later be incorporated into the city of New Orleans. The land had an old mansion on it, and the rest of the property was used as an orange grove. They constructed a new school on the land. In March 1887, the first building was formally dedicated. Southern's board of trustees and facility struggled through some difficult and uncertain days, but they persevered. In 1891, the federal government recognized Southern University as a land-grant college; thus, making it eligible for federal assistance.

In 1909, a growing number of Blacks in the rural areas of the state petitioned the governor to establish another university and to centrally locate it in the state. At this time, Joseph Samuel Clark, president of the Louisiana Colored Teachers Association (1908-1915) was a major advocate for the move. Their intent was to have the state legislature pass an act to establish a second institution for Black students, not relocate Southern University. Their second goal was to address the need for more Black teachers in the rural areas. On July 19, 1912, the governor signed an act to relocate Southern University outside of the city of New Orleans.

The move was opposed by the mayor and other elected officials of New Orleans, a large segment of the Black population, and especially the Catholic community. The Black Catholics wanted Southern to stay because it was the only nonsectarian university in New Orleans that Blacks could attend. The administration of Straight and New Orleans universities supported the move because it meant opportunities for them could grow. Some Black people felt that the normal school, which trained the school teachers, should be left in New Orleans because this was where the majority of the Black population lived, and yet others felt that the institution would not get adequate state funding; thus, Southern would be doomed to fail.

In 1914, in an effort to carry out the mandate of the legislature, the board of trustees appointed Joseph Samuel Clark president of the university (a post he would hold until his death 1938). They instructed him to seek a suitable location to relocate the school. On March 14, 1914, the state of Louisiana purchased an old 351-acre plantation in Scotlandville, north of Baton Rouge, for the new home of Southern University. Today, Southern University is the largest traditionally Black university system in the United States.

DILLARD UNIVERSITY

Dillard University was incorporated in the city of New Orleans on June 6, 1930. It is the end product of a cooperative enterprise of the American Missionary Association of the Congregational Church, the Board of Education of the Methodist Episcopal Church, the General Education Board, the Julius Rosenwald Fund, and the citizens of New Orleans. To carry out this effort, they had to raise two million dollars. The citizens of New Orleans contributed more than $242,000 through fundraisers. The school was named in honor of James H. Dillard, a former professor at Tulane University, who had served as president and director of the Jeanes Foundation for Negro Rural Schools.

The objectives and purposes were spelled out as follows: "to conduct an educational institution, including all educational and medical departments and hospitals...and to continue the work carried on by Straight University, founded by the American Missionary Association in 1869; New Orleans University, founded by the Methodist Episcopal Church in 1873, and Flint-Goodridge Hospital and Gilbert Academy all of which were merged to form Dillard University." Gilbert Academy of New Orleans, a feeder school, remained open until 1949.

The first unit of the newly formed Dillard University to be constructed was a new Flint-Goodridge Hospital, at an initial cost of one-half million dollars, which opened in 1932. In 1935, when Straight College and New Orleans University closed, Dillard University officially opened on September 24, 1935. Will W. Alexander was appointed acting president and Albert W. Dent as the business manager. William Stuart Nelson was later appointed the first president. Dent became the president in 1941. During Dent's administration, most of the nineteen buildings on the campus were built.

The campus of Dillard University was located on seventy acres of land in the Gentilly Road, within the city limits. Among some of the buildings on the campus are Edgar B. Stern Hall, named in honor of a member of the board of trustees and a benefactor; Will Alexander Library, named for a board of trustees; the science building and the Lawless Memorial Chapel, and the Gentilly Gardens Terrace living quarters for facility members were built by a great alumnus of Straight University, Dr. Theodore K. Lawless, the world-renowned dermatologist. Men and women dormitories and gymnasium were constructed and dedicated in the 1950s. Ms. Fannie C. Williams, a great educator and alumna, was also a benefactor for whom the women's dormitory was named. The Southern colonial style buildings and the trees on the campus were planned from the beginning. The architecture of the buildings is in the Georgian or modified classical tradition. All of the white buildings are built of stone and brick, with large columns.

Dillard took on the "Blue Devil" as its mascot. It developed an athletic program for the students, which included intercollegiate football, basketball, tennis, and golf to name a few. It awarded the baccalaureate degree in the arts and sciences, home economics, pre-medical, nursing programs.

As the institution began to take on its own identity, a clear vision of its philosophy and dedication to the community unfolded in its intentions: "the program of the undergraduate is designed for men and women who want to learn and lead—to learn with thoroughness and to lead with wisdom and understanding." And to this end, Dillard University continues to labor.

ARTHUR ESTÉVES
CIVIC LEADER AND PHILANTHROPIST

Arthur Estéves was born at Port-au-Prince, Haiti. At age three, his parents moved to New Orleans, Louisiana. He received his education in New Orleans. He was among the first Black to establish a sail-making business in New Orleans, and in later years, he joined partnership with one Mr. Fauna. Their firm, Estéves and Fauna, were among the most prominent sail-making and awning-making companies in New Orleans.

Arthur Estéves was associated with many charitable causes throughout the city. Before Reconstruction, Blacks in New Orleans received an education in private schools or by private tutors. Many wealthy Black families sent their children to Europe to get an education. In 1841, the New Orleans Public School System was established. That system did not accept Black pupils at that time, although Blacks paid taxes same as any other citizens for the support of the public schools. With monies bequeathed by Madame Marie C. Couvent the Catholic Indigent Orphans' Institute was established. In 1884, Mr. Estéves was selected to be president of the directors of the institute for indigent orphans. This body of civic-minded and philanthropic men provided the school with teachers, books, and other materials needed to sustain the school. The community had great respect for Mr. Estéves's honesty, philanthropy, and his commitment to justice and equality.

In 1890, a group of concerned Black citizens organized the Citizens' Committee. The mission of the Citizens' Committee was to challenge the adoption and enforcement of the state statutes that established the unjust laws that discriminated against the Black people in Louisiana. The focal point of their challenge became Act 111 of the 1890 State Legislature, a measure known as the Separate Car Law. At the first meeting of the Citizens' Committee, Mr. Estéves was selected to serve as its president. The committee gained the support of many citizens to challenge that law in the courts. In their challenge in the case *Plessey v. Ferguson* in 1896, the United States Supreme Court ruled in favor of a doctrine of "separate but equal" and against the Citizen's Committee. This was a devastating blow to the Black community of New Orleans. Following this case, Mr. Estéves declined in his public challenges of the state's segregationist legislation. Arthur Estéves died on January 28, 1908, and he was buried in St. Louis Cemetery #2.

FIRST AFRICAN BAPTIST CHURCH
2216 Third Street

During the early nineteenth century in Louisiana, when the French and Spanish cultures predominated, the Roman Catholic Church was the only religion sanctioned by law. The population consisted of Whites, free people of color, slaves, and Indians. Although the South was intensely proslavery, northern Whites traveled south to provide religious training for the Blacks and Indians.

In 1817, a group of twenty-two Blacks and sixteen Whites violated the law and met secretly to establish a church in a building on Canal Street. This group of Christians who followed the Baptist faith later moved to a location on St. Charles Ave. A few years later, the Blacks moved to a Burgundy Street site and established their own church, the first all-Black church in New Orleans. It was named First Baptist and later renamed First African Baptist. The pastor, Rev. Asa Goldburg, was the area's first Black pastor.

As the church prospered, the membership outgrew that building, and the congregation moved to Girod Street across from the Girod Street cemetery. After a few years on Girod Street, it settled into its present location on Third Street. Throughout the nineteenth century and into the twentieth, this church and the Wesley Methodist Church served as guides and inspiration to Black people of other denominations in New Orleans.

WESLEY UNITED METHODIST CHURCH
2517 Jackson Ave.

In 1802, the Methodist Church sent several evangelists to Louisiana to minister to all the people: Whites, Indians, and Blacks. They were greeted with strong opposition from the Catholic-dominated population of the Louisiana Territory; however, small groups of White Methodists ministered to Blacks and Indians while attempting to establish their first church in 1812.

In 1838, in a warehouse located on Gravier Street, between Carondelet and Baronne streets, Wesley United Methodist Church was founded by a group of free Blacks, Whites, and slaves. Together they were taught the doctrines and discipline of the Methodist Church, which had been established in Louisiana just eleven years prior. The first pastor was L. S. Scott, a White man. In the early church, the men sat on one side of the sanctuary and the ladies on the opposite side during the worship service, and the children sat around the railing of the altar.

The Methodist Church grew in popularity among Blacks, Whites, Creoles and Indians. In 1844, the Wesley Church moved to South Liberty Street, where its membership grew to more than five hundred. The slaves and free people of color built their first church with their own skills and labor, including making their own bricks. In 1863, the Emancipation Proclamation was read from the pulpit of the church. It was the proclamation issued by

President Abraham Lincoln which declared the freedom of all slaves in the territory. Many of the Blacks who became elected officials during the Reconstruction era worshiped here.

On Christmas Day 1865, a group of four White ministers and twelve Black ministers organized the Mississippi Mission Conference in Wesley Chapel. This organization included ministers from Louisiana, Mississippi, and Texas. All of the later Methodist Episcopal churches were established and sanctioned by this Mississippi Mission Conference, until the Louisiana Mission Conference subsequently was formed.

"Mother Wesley," as the church is affectionately known, has given birth to several other Methodist churches in the New Orleans area, including St. James AME, Grace United Methodist, and St. Mark Fourth Baptist Church.

In 1951, the church was forced to move because the City of New Orleans was developing a new civic center and a railroad terminal in that area. The congregation at that time united with Mount Zion Methodist Church to worship at 2517 Jackson Street. After the Mount Zion congregation built its new church, Wesley purchased the old church. Many notable people have visited this historic church, including civic leaders, church leaders, writers, historians, local politicians, and the twenty-fifth president of the United States, William McKinley.

FIRST STREET UNITED METHODIST CHURCH
2309 Dryades Street

During the days of slavery in New Orleans, slaves were permitted to congregate on an empty lot on the Faubourge Livaudais Plantation. It was on this site that a group of faithfuls met to give glory and praise to God. In 1833, these slaves acquired the land and constructed a small building that was used as their church. In 1845, this church was named Winans Chapel, in honor of one of the founders of the Methodist Church in Louisiana, and formed the beginning of the First Street Methodist Church. The building was later moved to the site where the present day Care Center is located. When the new sanctuary was constructed, it was patterned on the Christ Church Cathedral of St. Charles Avenue. Initially, the church operated under the jurisdiction and assistance of the Wesley Methodist Church. On August 15, 1877, the church became fully independent when the ownership was transferred from Wesley Chapel to the trustees of the First Street Methodist Church.

On August 30, 1894, under the leadership of the pastor, Rev. R. M. Davis, the congregation built a new parsonage and educational building. In 1920s the original church was destroyed by fire. Rev. Calvin Stanley and the congregation rebuilt the old structure, but that too was demolished, and they were left with a vacant lot; only the brick sanctuary remained. However, the congregation continued to worship God at other sites, and they made preparations to build a new edifice. In 1937, their prayers were answered: a new edifice and parsonage was constructed on the lot.

In 1984, under the pastorate of Rev. Abraham E. Davis, the church and all of the facilities were remodeled, and many programs have been initiated since to service the people of the community. To the credit and honor of the pioneers of this church, it has been placed on the register of historic landmarks.

THEODORE KENNETH LAWLESS
(DERMATOLOGIST, EDUCATOR, AND PHILANTHROPIST)
DECEMBER 6, 1892-DECEMBER 6, 1970

Theodore Kenneth Lawless was born in Thibodaux, Louisiana, on December 6, 1892, the son of Rev. Alfred and Harriet (Dunn) Lawless. He graduated from Straight College of New Orleans and several other colleges, obtaining several degrees in medicine and dermatology—his specialty. In 1924, Dr. Lawless began his practice in Chicago; that same year, he became an instructor in dermatology at Northwestern University, where he served until 1940. Though recognized as an excellent student and teacher, he experienced race prejudice. He conducted research in his specialty area in many foreign countries and published his finds in many leading medical journals. He was known as one of the world's leading skin specialists.

In 1940, Dr. Lawless began private practice; he invested his earnings and amassed considerable wealth. He founded an insurance company, a savings and loan association, and was successful in numerous other private ventures. As Dr. Lawless's financial resources grew, so did his philanthropic and humanitarian acts. He motivated the establishment of several dermatological clinics in the U.S., Israel, and Jerusalem. He established the Lawless Memorial Chapel and the Gentilly Apartments of Dillard University. He served on the board of trustees of Talladega, Houston-Tillotson, Roosevelt, and Rocky Mountain colleges, and Fisk and Dillard universities (president). In 1954 he became the thirty-ninth recipient of the Spingarn Medal of the NAACP. Throughout his career, he received many awards for his great medical and philanthropic contributions and for his love for mankind.

CHARLES "BUDDY" BOLDEN
SEPTEMBER 6, 1877-NOVEMBER 4, 1931

Charles "Buddy" Bolden was born in New Orleans on September 6, 1877. It is believed that Buddy began his education at the Fisk School for Boys. His first cornet lessons were taken from a neighbor, Manuel Hall. As Buddy's talent with the cornet developed, Charley Galloway hired him to play in his band. It wasn't until 1888 that Buddy realized his own possibilities and formed his own band.

Buddy worked days as a laborer until 1900, when he became successful enough as a musician and no longer needed a secondary income. He played within the boundaries of Storyville for about six years and his name became known citywide. Bolden's band was very much in demand, and they played all across town. Bolden's style of playing was easily recognized because he improvised as he interpreted a song instead of playing the music as written. His style was lively and flamboyant and was not popular among other musicians at that time. Buddy's popularity hit its peak around 1905, and that year, his musicians were listed in the city directory. Buddy Bolden reigned as king of New Orleans's Black music as a result of this music called jazz. Buddy took on more and more jobs to keep ahead of his competitors who had adopted his style of playing and were being as creative as he had originally been. Buddy began drinking heavily and could no longer keep the various elements of his world in their places. Around mid-1906, Buddy was suffering from bouts of insanity and on a downhill course. On April 4, 1907, Charles Bolden was declared insane and was committed to Jackson Insane Asylum of Louisiana. Buddy remained institutionalized for the last twenty-four years of his life. He died on November 4, 1931. The Boldens' home at 2309 First St. in New Orleans is still standing and was declared a historic district landmark in 1978.

FANNIE C. WILLIAMS
MARCH 23, 1882-JUNE 12, 1980

Fannie C. Williams was born in Biloxi, Mississippi, on March 23, 1882. She attended High School and College in New Orleans. In 1904, she graduated from Straight College and earned several other degrees in education. Aside from a few years teaching in Mississippi, Ms, Williams's entire professional career was spent in the public schools of New Orleans.

A pioneer in education, she dedicated her life to educating Black people as a classroom teacher and principal of Valena C. Jones Elementary and Normal schools. Her career in these schools spanned thirty-three years. She encouraged growth and the importance of excelling in all endeavors. She started many programs at Jones School, which affected children and teachers throughout the system, such as an annual health program which culminated in Child Health Day on May 1, a parent study group, a nursery school and kindergarten. Ms. Williams, an active professional and civic leader, served as president of the National Association of Bachelors in Colored Schools, participated in several White House conferences on child care and housing. She served on the board of trustees for Dillard University, Flint Goodridge Hospital, and as a member of many community organizations. After her retirement from the school system, she remained active in educating young people. During her lifetime, Fannie C. Williams received many honors in recognition of her contributions. Before her death on June 12, 1980, a women's dormitory on Dillard's campus was named in her honor.

WILLIAM H. MITCHELL
(EDUCATOR, PHILANTHROPIST, AND CIVIC LEADER)

William Henry Mitchell, Jr., was born in Princeton, New Jersey, on April 6, 1898. He received his early education in Princeton. He earned a bachelor of arts degree from Springfield College, which was noted for developing Young Men's Christian Association (YMCA) executives. He received a masters degree in economics from Columbia University in New York. In 1925, Mitchell moved to New Orleans to take over as executive director of the colored YMCA. Under his leadership, a new structure was erected, named Dryades Street YMCA. He also established the YMCA's School of Commerce, which offered business courses and secretarial skills.

During the 1940s, Mr. Mitchell traveled to the Republic of Liberia, Africa, to assist with the establishment of a YMCA there. While there, he recorded, on motion picture film, the people and living conditions of Liberia. When he returned to the United States, he toured the country with this film, raising money for the Liberian YMCA. His work was brought to the attention of the president of Liberia, who solicited him to become an honorary consul general of the Republic of Liberia at the port of New Orleans.

As honorary consul general, he would meet all Liberian registered ships carrying African students. He sometimes used his own money to care for some of the students. Often, he housed, fed, provided clothing, and paid tuition for some students when they were en route to northern schools. He placed others in New Orleans's universities with a clear understanding that his home was their home away from home.

Mr. Mitchell founded and directed the Spaulding Business Colleges, which was located in Mobile, Alabama; Shreveport and Baton Rouge, Louisiana. He intentionally did not locate a school in New Orleans because he didn't want any questions of impropriety or conflict with the YMCA's School of Commerce. During the 1950s, he was featured in an article in *Fortune Magazine*, and his private schools, as well as the YMCA's School of Commerce, were cited for excellence in curriculum and job placement performance. As executive secretary (director) of the Dryades Street YMCA in New Orleans, he instituted many educational and social programs for the youth of the community; additionally, he promoted business and trade between businessmen in New Orleans and the Liberians. During the 1940s and '50s, many of the graduates of the Dryades Street programs worked for the U.S. government and major companies throughout the nation.

On April 1, 1953, in the city of Monrovia, Liberia, Mr. Mitchell was appointed consul general of the Republic of Liberia at the port of New Orleans by William V. S. Tubman, president of Liberia. On May 13, 1953, U.S. President Eisenhower issued him his exequatur. Mr. Mitchell made all arrangements for the official state visit of President W. V. S. Tubman to New Orleans. President Tubman was received with official receptions.

William H. Mitchell died in New Orleans on February 2, 1957. The community lost a business leader and an educator. He succeeded in making the Dryades Street YMCA the focal point of the Black community and a source of education and leadership training for the young people.

ULYSSES GRANT DAILEY
PHYSICIAN AND EDUCATOR

Ulysses Grant Dailey was born on August 3, 1885, in Donaldsonville, Louisiana. While growing up in Louisiana, he was greatly influenced by his mother, to become a concert pianist and conductor. She taught him to play classical music on the piano. She taught him to be respectful of the Black leaders of his day.

His family later moved to Fort Worth, Texas while he was in high school. He was regarded as a bright and gifted student. A local physician who was a professor, in the Medical Department at Forth Worth University became interested in Ulysses' achievements. In 1902, he encouraged Grant to enter Northwestern Medical School in Chicago, Illinois. He graduated the youngest of fifteen students in his class. Ulysses experienced much discrimination against his race throughout his training, but he still remained focused on becoming a good physician.

From 1908 to 1912, he studied under the world renowned heart surgeon, Dr. Daniel Hale Williams. Dr. Dailey saw Dr. Williams as his role model as both surgeon and physiologist. He worked as an assistant surgeon to Dr. Williams. Dr. Dailey became a devoted member of the National Medical Association. He later became an associate professor at Providence Hospital. During this time, Dr. Dailey was published in the New York Medical Journal,

Dr. Dailey's writing skills were recognized by his professional peers, and he was appointed to the editorial board of the Journal of the National Medical Association. He served on that board from 1910 to 1943. In 1914, his surgical skills earned him another great honor. Dr. Dailey's peers elected him chairman of the Surgical Section of the National Medical Association. One year later, he was elected President of the National Medical Association.

In 1925, Dr. Dailey went to Europe to pursue more knowledge of surgical techniques and also to be relieved from the pressures of working in a highly racist situation. Frustrated by racial barriers and political problems within and outside Providence Hospital, Dr. Dailey decided to open his own hospital, freeing himself from the politics and policies, and philosophy that caused him much grief. He purchased 2 stone houses on the corner of 37th Street and Michigan Ave. in Chicago, Illinois. After remodeling the houses he named them The Dailey Hospital and Sanitarium.' Dr. Dailey was the hospital's Surgeon-in-Chief for six years. He was a frequent lecturer at Northwestern University, and Surgeon Emeritus at Providence Hospital. He co-founded the International College of Surgeons. Dr. Dailey became one of the first four Black members of the American College of Surgeons. He served as associate editor of the Journal of the National Medical Association for 38 years. Dr. Ulysses Grant Dailey died in Chicago, Illinois on April 22, 1961.

ORETHA CASTLE HALEY
(CIVIC, POLITICAL, SOCIAL LEADER, ADMINISTRATOR, AND EDUCATOR)

Oretha Castle was born on July 22, 1939, in Oakland, Tennessee. At age eight, Oretha Castle moved to New Orleans, Louisiana, with her family. She was educated in the public schools of New Orleans and Southern University at New Orleans. Oretha began a lifetime committed to the improvement of her community. As a teenager, in high school, Oretha became aware of the discriminatory practices against Black people in New Orleans. She became active in the fight for civic and social justice in her community against racist merchants. This led her to the pickets and sit-in demonstrations against merchants on Canal and Dryades streets. These efforts were organized by the Consumers League and the Congress of Racial Equality (CORE). Oretha served as the New Orleans's chapter and state president, working in the South to cause racial equality for Blacks.

It was during her work with CORE that Oretha met Richard Haley, also a fighter for civic and social justice. In 1967, they were married, and to this union, four children were born. Richard and Oretha were strong advocates of education and opportunities for Blacks in the local community. Oretha worked for two years as a community organizer with the anti-poverty program in New Orleans. Oretha Castle was a loving and caring person with strong convictions. She aggressively entered the fight against abusive police practices, also to desegregate segregated recreational facilities operated by the city and several other social injustices practiced against Black people. She organized many successful groups to register voters. Her work as an advocate for the right to vote and community participation ushered in several pioneering individuals to run for political offices. Her efforts further instigated the organizing of the Southern Organization for Unified Leadership (SOUL).

In the 1970s, Oretha Haley was appointed deputy administrator at Charity Hospital at New Orleans, where she removed barriers and opened opportunities for the poor and the afflicted. She also served as director of minority recruitment programs for the LSU Medical School. However, her enthusiasm to carry out her philosophies came closer to reality when she organized her own day-care center, the Learning Workshop. The children of the community were taken to a new height at the Learning Workshop. This early childhood center gave these youngsters a good educational foundation and a strong sense of racial identity and self-respect.

While working for the Urban League of Greater New Orleans, Oretha galvanized the uptown community against the state and federal government who wanted to destroy the Black community to build a bridge across the Mississippi River. Her courageous leadership on this issue prompted the founding of another political organization, Black Organization of Leadership Development (BOLD). Also, on the political front, Oretha Haley directed the campaign to successfully elect the first Black woman, Dorothy Mae Taylor, to the Louisiana State House of Representatives and, later, the office of council-at-large for New Orleans. Mrs. Haley also successfully directed the campaign to elect Gail Glapion to the Orleans Parish School Board. As a rooted citizen in her community, Oretha Castle Haley formed a social-action group of women called the Black Women's Assembly (BWA). This group and its members played a pivotal role in establishing policy for the Orleans Parish School Board and the appointment of a Black superintendent.

On October 10, 1987, the citizens of New Orleans were deeply saddened when this giant among civil-right leaders died. In honor of her many contributions to this community, on July 22, 1989, the City of New Orleans renamed Dryades Street to Oretha Castle Haley Boulevard, and the Orleans Parish School Board renamed the Charles Gayarre Elementary School to the Oretha Castle Haley Elementary School.

HENRIETTE DELILLE
PATRON AND RELIGIOUS LEADER
1813-NOVEMBER 1862

Henriette Delille was born in New Orleans in the year 1813. She was the youngest of three children born to Marie Joseph Dias, free woman of color, and Jean Baptiste Delille-Sarpy. As a child, Henriette was destined for the same lifestyle as that of her female ancestors, to be a mistress of some aristocratic White man. But instead, at age thirteen, she began to develop into a strong-willed individual, rebelling against the customs and lifestyle of her quadroon class. Just as many of the women of her class, Henriette received a good education and was instructed in nursing and housekeeping by her mother. She learned to prepare medicines for the sick using roots and herbs from this tropical environment.

During her teen years, Henriette was introduced to a French nun, Sister St. Marthe Fontier. Henriette was immediately impressed with Sister Fontier's piety and compassion for the souls of others. She wanted to do something which was not open to people of color: a total dedication to God and the Roman Catholic Church by vowing her life and her deeds to charity, the ignorant, the poor, and the sick. It was the lifestyle of the religious and total devotion to God and the needy which impressed her most. In the 1820s she met Juliette Gaudin, a young girl of Cuban descent; they shared the same principles and desire for a religious life. They often prayed together and labored among the needy.

Ms. Delille met another woman, Marie Aliquot, who was committed to supporting the slaves and the sick with her money and other resources. Ms. Aliquot and Pere Rousselon, the vicar general of the diocese, also helped to secure for them the formal acceptance by the Roman Catholic Church of a Black order of nuns.

Ms. Delille received the first inspiration to become a religious on the feast day of the Presentation of the Blessed Virgin Mary and, in 1852, received her first vows on the same feast day; thus, they called their group the Sisters of the Presentation. Later, they adapted the Holy Family (Jesus, Mary, and Joseph) as their patron, and thus, changed their name to the Sisters of the Holy Family.

On October 15, 1852, at the dismay of many family members and friends, Ms. Delille and two of her associates, Juliette Gaudin and Josephine Charles, made their first vows of the Catholic Church towards becoming nuns. Henriette was formally named the superior or the mistress of novices.

Ms. Delille, who was given the name of her grandmother Henriette, was able to use the wealth and educational privileges of her family. Friends and well wishers of the aristocratic class provided charitable assistance to the unfortunate members of her own race, slaves, and needy free people of color. Her grandmother purchased a piece of property on Rue d'Orleans, between Bourbon and Royal streets, near the St. Louis Cathedral, which would later become the home of this small-but-growing group of religious women. From these humble beginnings, the order of the Sisters of the Holy Family has established schools and nursing homes for the sick throughout the United States and in foreign lands. Their Christian works have attracted many young women to serving God and his people.

In 1988, the Sisters of the Holy Family were informed by the Vatican that they may proceed with the cause of canonization of Mother Henriette Delille. This is the beginning of the process by which a person is elevated to being named a saint. Mother Henriette Delille could well be the first Black North American to become a saint in the Roman Catholic Church.

SAINT MARK'S FOURTH BAPTIST CHURCH
2130 Perdido Street

Around the early 1850s, the Shepherd family moved to New Orleans from Virginia, bringing with them their slaves. Mr. Shepherd treated his slaves in accordance with the Louisiana law, which mandated that the slaves be given a religious instruction and upbringing, and the family, along with their slaves, attended the Coliseum Place Baptist Church. One of their slaves, Robert Henry Steptoe, showed a keen awareness and interest in this faith. The Shepherd family educated and gave him freedom because of his strong faith and desire to teach the doctrine of Christ. After much study and training, the pastor of the Coliseum Place Baptist Church ordained Robert H. Steptoe a minister in the Baptist Church.

In 1854, Rev. Steptoe organized a group of Black Christian followers into a church. The church house was given to them by his former masters, and this church was called St. Mark Street (now Magnolia Street) Fourth Baptist Church. In 1867 the church was incorporated, and Rev. Steptoe served the congregation as the pastor and spiritual leader until his death in 1884.

The church experienced many unfortunate circumstances, but this group of faithfuls was determined to worship God at St. Mark's, and they refused to be discouraged. In 1909, under the leadership of Pastor Jackson Acox, the membership and the financial stability of the church were enhanced, and new article of incorporation were executed.

In 1923, construction on the present edifice was begun at the corner of Galvez and Perdido streets. During the construction of the church, the members held services on the site. St. Mark's Fourth Baptist Church is currently celebrating sixty-five years in the present location. Rev. Robert Turner, the tenth successor to Rev. Steptoe, also serves as dean of the Union Baptist Theological Seminary.

ST. PETER AFRICAN METHODIST EPISCOPAL (AME)
1201 Cadiz Street

In 1850, in a small house shaded by a stand of stately oak trees, a group of free people of color came together to worship God. This historic house was located at Prytania and Valmont streets in Jefferson City (later incorporated into the city of New Orleans). The group was inspired by the teachings of Richard Allen, the founder and first bishop of the African Methodist Episcopal Church of Philadelphia, and they followed his religious teachings.

In 1858, this small group of African Methodists was allowed to worship in the nearby White Methodist Church of Jefferson, also located in Jefferson City. The institution's White congregation held services in the upstairs sanctuary, while the Blacks worshipped in the basement. Later, they would be permitted to worship in the balcony. The Blacks organized themselves as a separate congregation. During that year, a storm damaged the church, and the Blacks worked with the Whites to repair the church.

In the 1860s, the group made the decision to adhere more closely to the teachings of the African Methodist Episcopal Church of Philadelphia. As a result, they moved to another location nearby, choose their own pastor, and began holding their own services without the influence of the White Methodist leadership.

In 1867, under the pastorate of the Rev. Lazarus Gordon, they purchased land upon which they intended to build their own church. The growing congregation required more space immediately, and the board of trustees entered into negotiations with the White congregation of Jefferson Methodist Church for the "Church on the Hill." On March 31, 1877, the church was purchased for $4,000, and St. Peter AME held services upstairs in the sanctuary of its own church at 1201 Cadiz Street.

From these humble beginnings, the St. Peter church grew in faith and community service. In the early 1900s the church's basement was used as a school for Black youths studying practical nursing, secretarial, and business courses. It also served as an employment office during the Great Depression of the 1930s.

From this mother church, there would come several other churches in New Orleans, including St. Luke, St. Peter of Carrollton, and Mt. Zion churches. In 1979, this church was placed on the national register of historic landmarks.

GRACE UNITED METHODIST CHURCH
2001 Iberville Street

The family tree of the Grace United Methodist Church spans one hundred thirty-seven years, beginning in 1850 when the Mississippi Mission Conference established the Soule Chapel Methodist Church. Later, this church merged with the Marais Street Methodist Church to form the Pleasant Plains Methodist Church. The congregation was comprised of French, Sicilians, and Creoles. From the 1870s to 1917, the Pleasant Plains Church and Union Chapel shared the same pastor.

In 1917, the children attending Union Chapel, which was located on Bienville between Villere and Marais streets, were turned away by law officers because the church was located in the red-light district. Since the children of any church are an integral part to the continued growth of the church, the pastor, Rev. Hubbard Daniels, the area bishop, and the officers and members of Union Chapel and Pleasant Plains, which was located on Perdido Street, met to resolve the dilemma of Union Chapel. They voted to merge the churches and worship together. Initially, finding a place to worship was a serious problem for this group of faithfuls. The New Orleans School Board allowed the newly formed congregation to hold services in the Albert Wicker School building, and they later moved to a horse stable located on North Derbigny between Bienville and Conti streets.

This congregation exhibited great strength and courage to continue their efforts to worship God. In 1917, under the leadership of their pastor, Rev. B.T. Mc Ewen, they purchased a German Lutheran church on Bienville at Prieur Street as their new home. While worshiping together one night in their newly acquired home,"Grace" was suggested as the name of the church by Ms. Sarah Jones who expressed "it was through the grace of God that we have come into being and through his grace he would lead us further."Thus, the name was accepted. From First Grace Methodist, the name grew to Grace Methodist Episcopal, and now Grace United Methodist Episcopal Church. This church has been served by nearly one hundred dedicated pastors who ministered, preached, and converted many to the gospel of God.

GREATER LIBERTY BAPTIST CHURCH
1230 Desire Street

*I*n the year 1853, faith brought a small group of Christians to a shedlike house on the corner of Marais and Piety streets. Led by the Rev. A. Wyatt, this group came together to organize their own church. They organized and named their church Liberty Baptist Church. Determined to worship in their own church, they worked together to cultivate a strong spirit of fellowship, which provided a solid foundation for the church.

From these modest but faithful beginnings, the members of Liberty Baptist Church developed a strong family bond. The founding members taught the congregation to persevere. This perseverance has been evident over the past one hundred thirty years. Rev. Wyatt died while leading his church in worship, and the members appointed another pastor, Rev. Henry Thomas. Rev. Thomas died shortly after appointment. However, before his death, he changed the name of the church to Greater Liberty Baptist Church.

In 1930, the congregation experienced significant growth under the pastorate of Rev. Noah Copelin. His motto was "With Christ to help us, we need never fail. He will supply all your needs." Rev. Copelin, who would serve as pastor for thirty-nine years, was a builder. The church came of age under his dynamic leadership, as he increased the membership and the financial resources. And the church became involved in community affairs. At the time of his death in 1969, plans were underway to build a new edifice. In 1971 a new pastor, Rev. Melvin Clark, arrived and continued to build on the foundation laid by his predecessors. On Sunday, July 17, 1977, the congregation officially dedicated their new edifice at 1230 Desire Street. A week of services in honor of the accomplishments of this church was held as they commemorated one hundred nineteen years of dedicated service to God and the community.

WILLIAMS METHODIST CHURCH
7510 Pearl Street

*T*he Clinton Street Methodist Church was organized in 1866 under the Mississippi Mission Conference, from which the Louisiana Conference was organized in 1869. The church's first pastor was Rev. Emperor Williams. The first church building was destroyed by fire in 1869 but rebuilt in 1870. A pioneer and true man of the cloth, Rev. Williams was one of the founders of both the Mississippi and Louisiana Mission Conference, which was responsible for organizing both Black and White Methodist Episcopal churches in these states. Rev. Williams also was the founder and president of Sager-Brown Orphans Home in Baldwin, Louisiana. He secured the property upon which the Clinton Street Church was situated, and this new religion fast attracted a congregation under Rev. Williams's skillful spiritual leadership.

In 1894, when Rev. Williams passed away, the congregation renamed the church in his honor, Williams Methodist Episcopal Church. In that year, fire again destroyed the church, but again it was rebuilt by its persevering congregation. The church, located in Jefferson City, would survive many ordeals and contribute much to the community. In 1924, for example, its members organized and erected a clinic to provide medical care for the needy. The roster of the forty-two ministers who have served this congregation have contributed to the growth of its physical edifice and the spiritual growth of the community. Currently undergoing renovations, Williams United Methodist Episcopal Church this year celebrates one hundred twenty-two years of continued service.

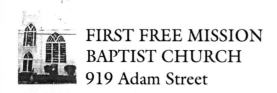

FIRST FREE MISSION BAPTIST CHURCH
919 Adam Street

The First Free Mission Baptist Church was organized on Burdette Street near Hampson Street in August 1868, by the Rev. Moses Johnson of Virginia. Shortly after the church was organized, however, he returned to Virginia. The church continued under the guidance of Rev. M. Allison for a short time and then under Rev. Guy Beck who served until 1888. The early years proved to be difficult years to keep a pastor, but in 1895, their eighth pastor, Rev. Houston, brought a new spiritual life to the church. New members and financial growth followed. After Rev. Houston passed away in November 1909, he was succeeded by several pastors who would serve only brief terms.

In 1911, the congregation elected a new pastor, Rev. Christopher Columbus Smith. On September 29, 1915, a storm destroyed the old church. This forty-seven-year-old congregation was determined to rebuild their church, and they did. After a year of praying, laboring, and raising money, they completed the new edifice. To this new structure, a parsonage was added. This edifice and the congregation have withstood many storms since 1915, and they have been blessed with a strong faith in God and good pastors to lead the flock. The church has become financially independent, and though it has been remodeled on several occasions, it continues to remain a vibrant house of God.

SECOND FREE MISSION BAPTIST CHURCH
1228 Burdette Street

The Second Free Mission Baptist Church was founded in 1869; the church was then known as First Free Mission Baptist. The first pastor was Rev. Moses Jackson, who ministered for only two years. During these early years, the church struggled through a fire which destroyed it and some disagreements within the Baptist community about the name, so the name was changed to Second Free Mission Baptist Church. The early pastors were all great preachers, and they inspired this growing congregation. Rev. H. C. Forster became the pastor in 1889, and during his tenure, much of the church's furnishings were acquired. Rev. Forster died in 1919, and the church suffered due to lack of strong leadership. There was dissension and a separation in the congregation, which resulted in the founding of Morning Star Baptist Church.

Rev. F. W. Scott took over as pastor, and the rebuilding of the congregation was evident by the erection of a church hall and a parsonage. In 1937, Rev. P. B. Fortner was selected as pastor. He was selected a second time in 1950 and served until his death in 1966. Rev. Fortner made significant contributions to the growth of the church and the saving of souls for God.

On March 30, 1967, Second Free Mission called on one of its own members, the Rev. Warren Joseph Ray, Sr. Rev. Ray was baptized in the church in 1941 and ordained to the gospel ministry in 1954. He taught in the Sunday school for over twenty-five years prior to his selection as pastor. Rev. Ray acquired considerable education and stressed the need for more knowledge of the church's teachings and involvement in the community to his congregation. Upon his death in 1973, his son, the Rev. W. J. Ray, Jr., was elected pastor to carry on God's work at Second Free Mission.

Rev. Ray met the challenge of his predecessors. Like his father before him, Rev. Ray grew up in Second Free Mission and was ordained by the same organization which ordained his father. Today, he carries on in his father's tradition of service: caring and ministering to the congregation. In addition, he has brought many innovations to the church. In 1980, the old church was demolished, and on May 18 of that year, a new edifice was dedicated to the glory of God. For one hundred eighteen years, Second Free Mission Baptist Church is still striving to build God's kingdom.

ST. JOHN INSTITUTIONAL MISSIONARY BAPTIST CHURCH
2538 Jackson Avenue

On May 23, 1869, Rev. Thomas Peterson, pastor of Zion Travelers Baptist Church, and a small group of Baptist pioneers set out to organize another Baptist church. The group elected

Rev. Joseph Jessup their first pastor; he would lead this new congregation for its first thirteen years. The group named their new church Saint John Fourth Baptist Church. The church was incorporated on May 23, 1871. At the death of Rev. Jessup, Rev. Joseph Tolbert was elected pastor. He was the spiritual leader for the next thirty-six years of growth and prosperity.

In 1918, under the pastorate of Rev. Frederick H. Collins, a new edifice was erected at 2434-36 First Street. After fifteen years of faithful service to the church and community Rev. Collins died. In 1933, the congregation elected Dr. Cleveland Charles Taylor from the youth group of the church to become its ordained minister. Dr. Taylor led the church to local and national prominence. His dynamic civic and religious leadership brought many positive assets to the church and its people, and the membership increased sharply. He established many church programs to foster the growth of the congregation, including a Vacation Bible School and educational scholarships for youth of the church to attend local universities. In 1945, the church purchased property on Jackson Ave. to build a new, larger edifice. On January 24, 1950, St. John Fourth Baptist Church was left without a pastor when Rev. Taylor expired.

The congregation then sent for one of its own, Rev. Willie Earl Hausey, who was then pastor of New Salem Baptist Church in South Bend, Indiana. Rev. Hausey brought many innovative ideas to St. John, which allowed for more participation by the membership. Rev. Hausey renovated the old church, whose congregation was rapidly outgrowing it. In 1955, under Rev. Hausey's leadership and the guidance of the Building Fund Committee, a larger, modern facility was constructed and a parking lot was added. After the new edifice and educational building were constructed, the name of the church was changed to St. John Institutional Missionary Baptist Church. During the past thirty-three years, Rev. Hausey has led St. John Institutional Missionary Baptist to many milestones.

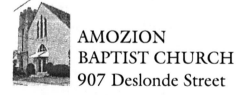

AMOZION BAPTIST CHURCH
907 Deslonde Street

Amozion Baptist Church was organized in October 1870, in a dairy on Crab Street (Burgundy Street) near Poland Avenue. (The name "Amozion" means I Love Zion.) On August 15, 1879, the present church site was purchased.

The first pastor, Rev. Charles W. Williams, was a student at Leland College at the time of the church's founding. After becoming pastor, he was elected president of the board of trustees and signed the act of incorporation of the church. A co-organizer of the First District Baptist Association, Rev. Williams was a pioneer in the Baptist Church for causes supporting Black people. Under his leadership, Amozion Baptist Church grew into a significant force in this community. Rev. Williams served Amozion for twenty-eight years, and several ministers of the gospel were ordained at Amozion under his spiritual guidance. These included Rev. Charles Sharkey and Noah Copelin, founder and pastor, respectively, of Greater Liberty Baptist Church, and Johnson Lockett, a community leader, for whom the Orleans Parish School Board named a school.

In 1919 Rev. B.A. Jolicoeur was elected pastor. He was an outstanding gospel preacher and is credited with leading many souls to church during his thirty years of service. The church was partially destroyed by fire in May 1937 and was remodeled in August of that year. As with his predecessors, Rev. Jolicoeur was an officer in the First District Baptist Association and the Louisiana Baptist Convention.

On November 10, 1949, Rev. L. C. Brooks was elected pastor. Rev. Brooks was christened and baptized in Amozion Baptist Church, and it was under his leadership that a new church was built. In November 1959, Mrs. B. A. Jolicoeur unlocked the door to the new Amozion edifice. After one hundred eighteen years of service to God and man, Amozion Baptist Church is still a viable force in this community.

MOUNT ZION UNITED METHODIST CHURCH
2700 Louisiana Avenue

*I*n 1870 a group of faithfuls came together to worship God and founded a mission station that was serviced by a "supply minister." Three years later, their first pastor, the Rev. James Haywood was appointed. Church services were held in the homes of the members at that time. Rev. Haywood immediately launched an effort that increased the membership and developed more comprehensive programs to serve church members and the community. With great difficulty, this congregation built their first church at 2517 Jackson Ave, a home they would share with other groups trying to organize a church.

Among the most progressive pastors to lead Mount Zion was Rev. W.T. Handy, who was a builder of services provided to the congregation. He revised the order of the services and initiated the idea of constructing a more modern edifice. During the ten-year leadership of Rev. Robert D. Hill, the present church located on Louisiana Ave. at Magnolia Street, was built and dedicated, and the old church was sold to Wesley United Methodist Church as an educational and activities center. In its new sanctuary, this proud congregation has played an important role in molding this community in Christian living.

CENTRAL CONGREGATIONAL UNITED CHURCH OF CHRIST
2401 Bienville Street

*I*n 1869, following the Civil War, the American Missionary Association (AMA) came to New Orleans to work among the freedmen and the free people of color in Louisiana. The AMA established Straight University on the corner of Esplanade and Derbigny streets. Straight University would later merge with New Orleans University to form the current

Dillard University. The chairman of the theology department at Straight University, Reverend Charles H. Thompson, DD, a Black man, met the Rev. Jacob A. Norager, pastor of a small group of worshipers who were dissatisfied being members of the congregation of St. James AME Church. This group of twenty-six women and six men from St. James AME, a few worshipers from Brown Congregational Church, and the Straight University Church organized Central Congregational Church on June 30, 1872.

In 1882, the AMA purchased a three-story building, the former Fourth Presbyterian Church building located on South Liberty at Gasquet (Cleveland) Street. This structure served as their home for sixty-two years. Because of the large size of the beautiful facility, the congregation adopted an open-door policy, and the church became the cultural center for the entire Black community of New Orleans. The largest meeting place in town, it was used for conventions, Masonic lodge meetings, dance recitals, and even a citywide banquet dinner for the great educator, Booker T. Washington.

In 1934, a wonderful era came to an end when the church was forced to move because the area had become highly commercial. The members held church services in the chapel of Straight University for ten years; later, they worshiped at Beecher Memorial Congregational for two years. In 1944, the church broke ground for its new home on the corner of Bienville and Tonti streets. On November 18, 1945, the new church was dedicated. The only remaining relic of the first church, the memorial bell, was placed on the front lawn and dedicated to the founders of the church.

The Orleans Parish School Board has honored five members of Central Congregational Church by naming a public school in their honor: Rev. Henderson H. Dunn, who served as pastor, and Florence J. Chester, both educators and co-organizers of the church's Isabell Hume Child Care Center (the first child-care center for Black children), Mary D. Coghill, L. B. Landry, and Fannie C. Williams. One member, Andrew Young, was elected mayor of Atlanta, Georgia, and many others have made outstanding contributions to society.

ST. JOHN DIVINE BAPTIST CHURCH
1763 No. Derbigny Street

*I*n 1873, in the home of a fellow Christian, a group of believers came together to worship God. This group of faithfuls formed the beginning of a congregation they would call the Samuel Israelite Baptist Church. The fledgling congregation was led by Rev. Charley Williams, a missionary minister from Amozion Baptist Church, who would later organize the Asia Baptist Church. Under his guidance, the congregation's numbers increased, and soon, a larger meeting site was needed.

On November 20, 1880, under the leadership of Rev. Louis Cass, they purchased their first permanent place to worship. When they acquired the new building, they also took on a new name: St. John Divine Baptist. Through the years, this congregation would grow in faith and finance, building a strong bond with local and national Baptist organizations and flourishing. On September 10, 1961, the last service was held in the nineteenth-century edifice. On November 5, 1961, they held a groundbreaking ceremony for a new church, and on November 25, 1962, the St. John Divine Baptist Church was rededicated to God.

On April 11, 1973, Rev. Louis W. Smith was installed as the eleventh pastor to lead this flock. Under his leadership, this church became known as "the church where hospitality and spirituality blend."

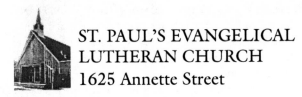

ST. PAUL'S EVANGELICAL LUTHERAN CHURCH
1625 Annette Street

In the summer of 1877, the Evangelical Lutheran Conference of North America elected to begin a mission for Blacks of the South. Their first mission and Sunday school was established in New Orleans in 1878. On March 9, 1879, on the corner of Allen Street and North Claiborne Avenue, a small chapel-school was dedicated to the glory of God as Evangelical Lutheran St. Paul's Chapel-School. Established to provide a basic education and instruction in the Christian faith, the school experienced many early problems with acceptance and was near closing several times for lack of students.

On May 29, 1881, Rev. Bakke, pastor of Mt. Zion Lutheran Church, organized the St. Paul's Lutheran Church. He provided religious instruction to the first confirmation class of three members, who became the first members of the church.

The new church increased in membership, soon outgrowing its small facilities, and in 1883, property was purchased at 1625 Annette Street to build a new church and school. Five years later, the congregation dedicated its new church to the glory of God in a large celebration. In 1889, a new school accommodating one hundred fifty students was dedicated.

In 1903, the Synodical Conference provided funds for the erection of Luther College on the grounds of St. Paul's, creating the first Black college established by the Lutheran Church. The pastor of St. Paul's became the president of the college, which operated intermittently for twenty-three years until it was closed permanently by the Depression of 1932. The Depression brought the members of this congregation closer together to save and care for their church. In 1941, the mission board sold the church to the congregation and gave them the land upon which the college had been situated.

At its seventy-fifth anniversary, this well established and growing congregation decided to demolish the old church, school, and college buildings to erect a larger church and school for the children. On February 7, 1965, the new church and school was dedicated, and today, St. Paul Evangelical Lutheran Church lives on in this community after one hundred-four years of teaching the word of God.

ISRAEL
BAPTIST CHURCH
1701 Marais Street

The Israel Baptist Church of New Orleans was organized and built in 1882, under the leadership of the Rev. Moses Gregg. Rev. Gregg led his congregation into the formative years of the church and pastored for twenty-six years. At the death of Rev. Gregg, the Rev. S. E. Piersey, pastor of Amozion Baptist Church, came in to serve until the Rev. Jake Thomas was elected pastor. But the next few years were uncertain ones for this struggling congregation. The second era of transformation for Israel Baptist Church began with the election of Rev. W. B. Williams after several pastors had brief periods with the church.

Rev. Willie Ben Williams, who was baptized in Israel Baptist Church, was elected pastor in 1920. He was an outstanding pastor for eighteen years while he renovated the church, increased the congregation, and promoted a healthier atmosphere for growth in their church. In 1939, Rev. Horace Brown was called to the pastorate, but his stay was short and filled with dissension. When he left, he departed with some of the members, and together, they established Galatia Baptist Church; however, the dedicated members of Israel Baptist Church continued to push on, doing the work of the Lord.

In 1941, another era of building and transformation was ushered in with the election of Rev. Halley Moses Willis as pastor. His vision was to build a new Israel. In 1944, they adapted a motto, "A New and Greater Israel," and embarked on building a new edifice. The last service was held in the old church on January 28, 1952; the church was demolished the next day. On Sunday, October 5, 1952, the congregation marched from St. Peter Baptist Church, where they had been holding services, to their new edifice at 1701 Marais Street. This congregation had much to be proud of, and Rev. Willis's dedication message said it all: "For we are assured that the victory lies not in our own strength or wisdom, but how closely we walk with God who is guiding us, WE GIVE THANKS!"

HAVEN UNITED
METHODIST CHURCH
8514 Plum Street

Haven Methodist Church was founded in 1883 by Rev. Madison C. B. Mason, pastor, and Louis P. Cushman, presiding elder. The church building was purchased from the Carrollton German Methodist Episcopal Church South for $1,000. Incorporated on March 24, 1897, it was named Haven Methodist Episcopal Church of Carrollton in honor of Methodist Bishop Erastus O. Haven. This church structure was renovated several times before it was demolished. In 1927, under the leadership of Rev. J. B. Johnson, the church was replaced with a stucco building, a sanctuary called the Uptown Lighthouse of Faith.

The congregation had a unique way of raising money while promoting Christian fellowship. Professor L. R. Scott organized Haven's Ship of Zion, performing a drama in their church as well as others using the front of a ship as the main stage prop. The participants sang hymns and performed skits based on the ship of Zion.

In the early twentieth century, Haven organized its own school for children up to fourth grade. It was one of the first schools in the Carrollton area open to Black children.

As if to test their faith, in July of 1981, the second church burned to the ground. One year later, construction began on the new sanctuary, and on February 13, 1983, the congregation entered the third church to occupy this same corner.

FIRST EMMANUEL BAPTIST CHURCH
1829 Carondelet Street

The First Emmanuel Baptist Church was founded in late 1886 by a small group of Blacks under the leadership of Rev. J. M. Richards, Sr. They held services in a blacksmith shop on South Peters Street and incorporated their church in the late 1880s. They purchased property at 432 Erato Street to build an edifice. All of the members of the congregation, including Rev. Richards, labored to build the first church structure there in 1889. When Rev. Richards died in 1909, his son, Rev. J. M. Richards, Jr., succeeded him. Rev. J. M. Richards, Jr., served the church until his death in 1918. The church's other pastors are Rev. Johnny Richards, Rev. Author Jones, Rev. Colberty Pye, and the current pastor, Rev. Samuel Hadley, who was elected pastor in April 1957.

Under Rev. Hadley's pastorship, First Emmanuel Church moved to a new location on Carondelet Street in 1962. On January 8, 1967, the Louisiana Grand Master of the Free and Accepted Masons laid a cornerstone to this edifice. Under Rev. Hadley's leadership, the church has assumed a dedication and commitment to youth community service as evident by the large number of young people in the church.

FIRST ZION BAPTIST CHURCH
7201 Olive Street

On December 1, 1887, the Reverend Stevens Bryant and a few faithful who wanted to follow the Baptist religion met and organized the Tin Top Church, located on the corner of Lafayette and Liberty streets. During the next twenty years, the church operated under five different pastors. Around the turn of the century, new quarters were needed, and the congregation met in the home of Brother Bud Peterson on Pine Street. In 1908, under the pastorate of Rev. D. B. Fisher, the flock moved several times to temporary homes. Also at this time, the congregation decided on a more fitting name for their church—First Zion Baptist Church.

Proud of their new name, the congregation built a new church and permanent home. Between 1908 and 1922, the church was destroyed three times, twice by fire and once by the terrible storm of 1915. But these acts taught the congregation humility and only deepened their faith in God. After a 1922 fire, the church services were held in the basement of the Danneel School. In November 1934, Rev. Fisher, their loyal pastor, died and was succeeded by his son, Rev. David Richard Fisher, who would serve the First Zion Baptist Church until his death in 1951. He contributed much to the financial growth and independence of the church.

For the next thirty-five years under the Rev. Norwood Thompson, Sr., significant growth and increased fellowship were ushered in. Following his father's death in December of 1984, Rev. Norwood Thompson, Jr., became pastor, bringing dynamic leadership to the church. Under his guidance, a new edifice was constructed, and the descendants of the Tin Top Church celebrated one hundred years of devotion to God and service to man.

INDEX

Alphabetical Listing

Field of Endeavor

Buildings, Institutions, and Organizations

Page locators following an entry that ends in numerals are italicized.

A

Amozion Baptist Church, 145-46
Autocrat Social and Pleasure Club, 94-95

C

Central Congregational United Church of
    Christ, 146

D

Dillard University, 121
Dryades Street Branch, New Orleans Public
    Library, 97

E

Economy Hall, 100-101

F

First African Baptist Church, 124
First Emmanuel Baptist Church, 150
First Free Mission Baptist Church, 117, 143
First Street United Methodist Church, 125
First Zion Baptist Church, 150-51
Flint-Goodridge Hospital, 121

G

Grace United Methodist Church, 141
Greater Liberty Baptist Church, 142, 145

H

Haven United Methodist Church, 149

I

Israel Baptist Church, 149

K

Knights Of Peter Claver Building, 23

L

Leland College, 117

M

Martin Luther King Walk and Monument,
    83
Milne Boys Home, 55, 91
Mount Zion United Methodist Church, 146

P

Pythian Temple, 110-11

S

Saint Augustine Roman Catholic Church,
    103
Saint Mark's Fourth Baptist Church, 140
San Jacinto Social and Pleasure Club, 101,
    112-13
Second Free Mission Baptist Church, 144
Sisters of the Holy Family, 25, 103, 106-7,
    139
Southern University, 114, 119
St. James Chapel African Methodist
    Episcopal Church, 109
St. John Berchman Asylum, 25
St. John Divine Baptist Church, 147-48
St. John Institutional Missionary Baptist
    Church, 144-45
St. Louis Cemetery No. 2, 91, 107, 123
St. Paul's Evangelical Lutheran Church, 148
St. Peter African Methodist Episcopal, 140
Straight University, 105, 146-47

W

X